111 Places in Edinburgh That You Shouldn't Miss

emons:

Cäcilienstraße 48, 50667 Köln
info@emons-verlag.de

Design: Eva Kraskes, based on a design
by Lübbeke | Naumann | Thoben
Edited by Cambridge Editorial, www.camedit.com
Maps: altancicek.design, www.altancicek.de
Printing and binding: sourc-e GmbH
Printed in Europe 2025
ISBN 978-3-7408-2575-1
Revised seventh edition, May 2025

Guidebooks for Locals & Experienced Travellers
Join us in uncovering new places around the world at
www.111places.com

Foreword

For centuries, writers have been fascinated by the contrasts of Edinburgh – its towering tenements and classical temples, rugged uplands and orderly gardens, claustrophobic wynds and panoramic vistas – darkly dour one minute and stunningly romantic the next. High culture thrives alongside low life – and even the weather is notoriously fickle. This guide takes its cue from that unpredictability. The 111 entries (and their accompanying tips) include hidden corners and unexpected sights little known even to long-term residents. The book also looks at some conspicuous local landmarks, telling the less familiar stories behind them – in the authentic rather than the mythologised versions. Readers will find many surprises close to the well-worn tourist trails, and others that take them into the suburbs and hinterland, all accessible on one of the best public transport systems in the UK.

Like so many 'must-visit' destinations around the world, Edinburgh is increasingly afflicted by the blight of overtourism. Many popular locations have already lost the very qualities that once made them special, thanks to constant processions of selfie-baggers obsessively ticking off lists of 'most instagrammable spots' or plodding in the imaginary footsteps of fictional characters, and ill-informed tour guides declaiming travesties of the city's history to their gullible followers. This regrettable state of affairs calls to mind a saying of Muriel Spark's immortal creation Miss Jean Brodie: 'For those who like that sort of thing, that is the sort of thing they like.'

If, however, you're an independent-minded individual keen to look beyond the superficial, the over-hyped and the spurious, and delve instead into the true character of this multi-faceted metropolis, this book is for you. I hope you enjoy discovering my personal selection of places, and exploring them at your leisure.

Gillian Tait

111 Places

1 21st Century Kilts

Skirts for men of the new millennium

The everyday menswear of the ancient Egyptians was the kilt, and similar types of attire were the norm for adult males in other parts of the world way before the invention of trousers. Nowadays, however, they're seen as a purely Scottish phenomenon – the tartan 'skirt for men' is a key element of traditional Highland costume, and probably the country's most famous cultural icon. There are shops all over the capital selling kilts, highly reputable establishments as well as shoddy purveyors of 'tartan tat'. But for would-be wearers seeking a quality garment with a unique contemporary twist, there's only one place to go: Howie Nicholsby's 21st Century Kilts.

Howie is a man with a mission: to rehabilitate the kilt as a normal item of clothing for modern men. Like a true evangelist, he practises what he preaches – he gave up trousers long ago, at the age of 21, and hasn't worn them since. An expert tailor, Howie learned the art of cutting, stitching, and pleating the six-plus metres of cloth required for a genuine kilt as an apprentice in his parents' business on the Royal Mile. He was just 18 when he first branched out on his own, keen to go back to basics by redesigning the more restrictive aspects of the formal garment to make it more comfortable and easier to wear. He also introduced detachable pockets – much more practical than the traditional sporran – and designed his own trademark kilt pin in the shape of a lightning bolt. Above all, he liberated kilts from tartan, seeing no reason not to make them out of a more versatile range of fabrics including denim, leather, pinstripe worsted and Harris Tweed.

After a decade building his brand from a base in the New Town, Howie moved back to his roots at Geoffrey (Tailor), the family business, where – aided by Fonzie, his adorable Border terrier/Bichon cross – he works alongside John Webster, a long-time specialist in traditional Highland dress. Bespoke kilts take up to eight weeks to make, but a ready-to-wear selection is always available.

Address 59 High Street, EH1 1SR, +44 (0)7774 757222, www.21stcenturykilts.com | Getting there Lothian Buses 35 to High Street, or 3, 29, 30, 31, 33 or 37 to South Bridge | Hours Mon–Sat 10am–5pm | Tip If you're looking for fine quality, expertly crafted knitwear, scarves, coats, blankets and home accessories with an authentic Scottish provenance, you'll find an excellent selection at Scottish Textiles Showcase, a couple of minutes' walk away at 20 St Mary's Street.

2 Abbey Strand

The privilege of sanctuary

At the very end of the string of streets that make up the Royal Mile, the boundary of Abbey Strand is discreetly marked by a trio of S-shaped brass studs on the roadway. Once you cross the line, you have the right – never revoked – to claim immunity from arrest, for this is an ancient place of sanctuary. Behind the gates ahead are the ruins of Holyrood Abbey, which like other medieval churches offered protection within its grounds to fugitives from the law. In later centuries, most of the desperate men who applied for sanctuary were guilty of nothing more than being unable to pay their bills, which up until 1880 was a very serious offence, punishable by imprisonment. Holyrood Abbey's estates originally stretched far and wide, encompassing Arthur's Seat and Duddingston, but it was on the pocket of land by its gates that the majority of these debtors chose to stay.

Their public humiliation began at the Castle, where they were 'put to the horn' with three blasts of a trumpet. To be granted sanctuary at Holyrood, they had to apply formally to the Bailie, pay a fee, and find a place to sleep within 24 hours of their arrival, but after that they were safe from prosecution, and life at Abbey Strand doesn't seem to have been all that bad for these transgressors. A small township crowded with lodging houses and taverns grew up to accommodate their needs; a couple of these buildings, 16th century in origin, still stand. Locals referred to the debtors as 'Abbey Lairds'; many of them were respectable lawyers, doctors and clergymen, and in the 1830s residents included the deposed King Charles X of France, and the opium-addicted writer Thomas de Quincy. Since Scots law didn't allow legal proceedings on Sundays, they even had the freedom to leave for 24 hours from midnight each Saturday – one minister used the time to return to his parish and deliver a weekly sermon.

Address Abbey Strand, EH8 8DU; at the foot of the Royal Mile | **Getting there** Lothian Buses 35 to Holyrood | **Tip** Don't miss the delightful garden behind the buildings. Opened in 2020, it was created as an educational resource, with plantings inspired by three phases in the history of the Holyrood site. Just beyond is the so-called Queen Mary's Bath House, a quirky little 16th-century building that may have been a tennis pavilion. A fanciful legend claims that Mary, Queen of Scots, bathed here in sparkling wine.

3 Ann Street

Homes of quality

The poet and conservationist Sir John Betjeman described it half a century ago as Britain's most attractive street, and the elegant Ann Street is still regularly named as one of the most desirable places to live in the whole of the UK. This secluded enclave of grand Georgian houses with extensive front gardens was the vision of the great Scottish portrait painter, Sir Henry Raeburn, who started to develop the site, then on the outskirts of the city, in 1813. Despite beginning life as a poor orphan, Raeburn had a meteoric rise to fame, and at 22 married a wealthy young widow, Ann Edgar. She owned the large acreage that became known as the Raeburn Estate, and the first street to be built there was named in her honour.

There is a surprising connection between this exclusive address and an enduringly popular brand of confectionery. In 1936, the Yorkshireman Harold Mackintosh had the novel idea of producing boxes of individually wrapped chocolates and toffees for the mass market. He named the brand 'Quality Street', after an immensely successful, twice-filmed play by J. M. Barrie, and packaged them in a tin (fondly remembered by those of a certain age) illustrated with two of its characters, a young lady and a soldier in Regency garb, stepping out together on the eponymous street.

The original model for Barrie's play was said to be none other than Ann Street, which he knew from his student days in Edinburgh. The author, who would go on to write *Peter Pan*, was inspired by its genteel charm to imagine the polite society who might have lived there in the early 19th century, creating an entertaining tale of restrained amorous pursuit and mistaken identities. Today's residents of the real-life Ann Street still appreciate the privileged seclusion of their village-like community, their only collective frustration being the shortage of parking spaces for their many horseless carriages.

Address Ann Street, EH4 1PL | **Getting there** Lothian Buses 36 to Dean Park Crescent (Ann Street) | **Tip** Just round the corner from this highly desirable enclave is a house that was once one of the city's most notorious addresses: 17 Danube Street, where from the late 1940s to the 1970s the infamous Dora Noyce ran a well-known and very successful brothel.

4__Ashley Terrace Boat House

Reviving the mathematical river

Edinburgh may not straddle a great river, but it does have two significant waterways meandering through it – the Water of Leith, and the long-neglected Union Canal. Now regenerated for the new millennium as a leisure facility, the canal offers a refreshingly different perspective on the city, for walkers and cyclists as well as all those who enjoy messing about in boats.

The Union Canal runs for almost 32 miles from Lochrin Basin, through the west of the city and out to the town of Falkirk. It was originally designed to transport coal and lime into the capital and, crucially, to join up with the existing Forth and Clyde Canal, thereby linking Edinburgh with Glasgow and the west coast. To make it speedier, it was constructed without locks as a contour canal, following a winding course at a constant 73 metres above sea level, which led to its nickname of 'the mathematical river'. It opened in 1822 after only four years' work, though it went seriously over budget, partly due to the expense of erecting three massive navigable aqueducts. Despite initial commercial success, the canal's heyday was short-lived – the opening in 1842 of the first railway to Glasgow greatly reduced its profitability. It gradually sank into disrepair, and was formally closed in 1965.

Twenty years later, the Edinburgh Canal Society was formed to lead the campaign for its reopening. One of their first projects was the complete refurbishment of an attractive old boathouse, to serve both as their headquarters and as a base for hiring out rowing boats. Resited by the bridge at Ashley Terrace, it soon became a popular landmark for all canal enthusiasts. Work on the Union Canal restoration began in 1991, and the bold ambition of restoring the link to Glasgow was finally realised in 2002, with the opening at its western end of a unique, vast boat lift known as the Falkirk Wheel.

Address by Lockhart Bridge, Ashley Terrace, EH11 1RS, www.eucs.org.uk | Getting there Lothian Buses 10 or 27 to Gray's Loan, or 38 to Ashley Terrace | Tip The boathouse is also the base of Scotland's oldest existing canoe club, Forth Canoe Club, which offers regular sessions of paddling on the canal from April to October for all levels, including beginners; see www.forthcanoeclub.co.uk for details.

5 Barnton Quarry Bunker

Cold comfort in the Cold War

The dark shadow of the Cold War, when the world was threatened with nuclear annihilation, loomed over people's lives for over 40 years. Fortunately for us all, the war never actually turned hot, and most of the scars it left, like the Berlin Wall, have been erased. To see the main material evidence of its consequences, we now have to look underground.

The bunker at Barnton Quarry brings this whole frightening period of recent history back into sharp focus. Its size alone – over 2,700 square metres – shows quite clearly how real and imminent the threat of a Soviet nuclear attack once was. During the 1950s and 1960s the UK government secretly constructed hundreds of subterranean complexes, including 14 regional seats of government (RSGs) from where ministers, civil servants and the military would have run the country, safe from nuclear fall-out. The Barnton RSG had room to accommodate more than 300 officials, as well as the late Queen Elizabeth and her household in the event of an attack occurring while she was in residence at Holyrood.

The quarry site had been a command centre for the RAF during World War II. For the RSG this was extended into a mini-city on three floors, 30 metres under Corstorphine Hill, with 3-metre-thick concrete walls and a complex air filtration system. Most large-scale bunkers were in the countryside, but this one's location on the edge of the city meant that locals got to know about it, and after it was decommissioned in the 1980s it was looted and damaged by vandalism. In 2011, however, it was bought by Cold War historian James Mitchell with the aim of opening it as a museum. Restoration work is still ongoing, but visitors will one day be able to tour reconstructed facilities including the military operations room, telephone exchange, BBC radio studio and living quarters, all vividly evoking the chilling 'what if' scenario of the attack that never came.

Address Clermiston Road North, EH4 7BN, www.barntonbunker.com | **Getting there** Lothian Buses 21 or 200 to Clermiston Road North; access to the bunker site is from the car park on the east side of the road | **Hours** Hard hat guided tours Sat 1pm; booking essential. New volunteer workers always welcome – see website | **Tip** Corstorphine Hill, to the east and south of the quarry, is a wooded nature reserve whose attractions include a tower built as a memorial to Sir Walter Scott, and a walled garden.

6 Blackford Hill

A ringside view of the Ice Age

Though some weary sightseers would maintain that this city is nothing but hills, Edinburgh is traditionally said to built on just seven: Arthur's Seat, the Castle Rock, Blackford, Calton, Corstorphine, Craiglockhart and Braid Hills. There are splendid views from all of them, but the most spectacular has to be the 360-degree panorama from the summit of Blackford Hill, which takes in the other six and much else beyond. This wild and windswept site offers an exhilarating escape from the urban jungle into what can seem not just another place, but a different era.

Under the racing clouds of a bright and breezy day, the city's topography is thrown into sharp relief, illustrating the ancient geological formations as if in a giant diorama. The built environment recedes into insignificance as you watch the ever-changing light reveal a landscape shaped millions of years ago by the action of ice. The most immediately striking features are the 'crag and tail' formations. These are studs of very hard rock, usually the cores of ancient volcanoes like the Castle Rock and Arthur's Seat, eroded and exposed by immense glaciers that left long tapering ridges of softer debris in their wake. The evidence of this momentous upheaval is made all the more vivid when you realise that the hill you're standing on is itself crag-and-tail shaped, formed like the others by a vast easterly moving iceflow.

In fact Blackford played a historic role in the understanding of glaciation. On the south side, by an old quarry, is a plaque commemorating the visit in 1840 by the pioneering Swiss-American geologist Louis Agassiz, the first person to recognise the visible effects of ancient ice sheets. On examining the grooved and polished surface of the rock face, he made the revolutionary declaration 'That is the work of ice!' Agassiz went on to formulate the earliest theory of the Great Ice Age.

Address Blackford Hill, EH9 3HJ | **Getting there** Lothian Buses 38 to West Mains Road (Royal Observatory), then walk up Observatory Road. For details of other routes, and walks around the hill, see www.fohb.org | **Tip** The copper-domed Royal Observatory, situated on the hill, holds regular public astronomy evenings and talks; see www.roe.ac.uk for details.

7 The Botanic Cottage

An enlightening garden centre

The newest building in the Royal Botanic Garden – known to all as the Botanics – is also the oldest. The freshly plastered, 250-year-old Botanic Cottage opened to the public in May 2016, after having been dismantled stone by stone, moved from the location where it had long lain derelict, and painstakingly reconstructed at Inverleith. The cottage was originally built at the entrance to the 'Physick Garden', just off Leith Walk, on land that is now Haddington Place. In 1763 John Hope, the Regius (Royal) Keeper – one of the most significant figures in the Botanics' history – secured this greenfield site to bring together the collections of the city's two existing physic gardens, which were being damaged by smoke pollution. The earliest of these had been established in 1670 in a small yard near Holyrood; within a few years this was extended to a larger site nearby, later to be covered by Waverley Station.

The original purpose of these gardens was to cultivate medicinal herbs and investigate their healing potential. John Hope trained as a physician, but his main interest was in plants and their physiology. His key aim in developing the new site was to set up a teaching institute for the emergent science of botany, so the garden cottage he commissioned included a classroom on the upper floor as well as living accommodation downstairs. Hope's lectures there inspired a generation of doctors and naturalists, establishing him as a major figure of the Scottish Enlightenment.

In the 1820s the Botanic Garden underwent yet another move, to Inverleith. The cottage remained on Leith Walk, surviving many changes of use and threats of demolition. Now, reincarnated in its rightful home, and beautifully restored, it is again fulfilling its educational function, enabling people of all ages and backgrounds – a much wider public than Hope could have ever dreamt of – to learn about the wonders of botany.

Address Royal Botanic Garden, Inverleith Row, EH3 5LR, +44 (0)131 248 2909, www.rbge.org.uk | **Getting there** Lothian Buses 8, 23 or 27 to Inverleith Row (Botanics) entrance also on Arboretum Place (though no buses go there); the Cottage is in the Demonstration Garden, in the western corner | **Hours** Garden: Mar–Sept 10am–6pm, Feb & Oct 10am–5pm, Nov–Jan 10am–4pm. For the educational programme in the Cottage, see website | **Tip** At the west gate on Arboretum Place is the John Hope Gateway, the Garden's interpretation centre. It has exhibitions, book and plant sales, and a restaurant, open daily from 10am, which uses produce from the gardens in its menus.

8 Bruntsfield Links

Play the course as you find it

Golf can be an exclusive and expensive pursuit, but there's one place in this city where it is neither. The rolling green sward of Bruntsfield Links, a public park just south-west of the Old Town, has a course that can be played by anyone, novices included, free of charge. And if you don't have your own clubs and balls, you can rent them at the '19th hole' for a modest fee.

Not only is this a delightfully scenic place to practise your swing, it's also an extremely historic one. The game, a Scottish invention, was already popular by the mid-15th century, and the open ground of the Links, at the eastern end of the Borough Muir, is one of the earliest documented locations where it was played. Rather inconveniently, it was also, for over two centuries, the site of stone quarries. However, such was the passion of citizens for the game that the council ruled many times that 'digging for stanes' would be allowed only on condition that it didn't interfere with 'the Gowf'. The course attracted all types of enthusiasts, from the medical student Thomas Kincaird, whose 1687 diary includes the earliest known instructions for playing the game, to the 18th-century New Town publican Alexander McKellar, who spent nearly every day on the course, having his meals brought out to him, and playing at night by the light of a lantern. Nor was it exclusively the province of men: a newspaper article of 1738 gives an account of a match here between two ladies, whose husbands acted as caddies; it was won by 'the charming Sally'.

Many golfing societies were founded and based at Bruntsfield, and during the 19th century overcrowding became a serious issue. New courses were eventually laid out in the suburbs to accommodate these clubs, and in the 1890s the site was turned from a six-hole links into a unique 36-hole short hole course, which has been open to all ever since.

Address Bruntsfield Links, EH10 4HR, www.bruntsfieldshortholegolfclub.co.uk | **Getting there** Lothian Buses 11, 15, 16, 23, 36 or 45 to Whitehouse Loan | **Hours** 36-hole course open daily late Apr–late Sept; 9-hole course open in winter; details posted at the 'green hut' kiosk | **Tip** Clubs and balls can be hired from the nearby Golf Tavern, 30–31 Wright's Houses; see www.golftavern.co.uk for details. This pub, whose origins go back to 1456, is also a comfortable place to relax with a drink after your exertions.

9 The Café Royal

A palace of a pub

Just behind the city's main shopping thoroughfare, now a sad shadow of its former self, are two of the most sumptuous rooms in Edinburgh. A minute's walk from the east end of Princes Street, up Gabriel's Road (the tail end of what was once a long country lane) takes you to the elegant *fin-de-siècle* realm of the Café Royal.

Before the mid-19th century, the many taverns of the city were mostly inconspicuous places, windowless dens in cellars or down narrow alleys. With the introduction of legislation controlling the sale of liquor, the drinking scene gradually changed, and the late Victorian era saw the emergence of 'palace pubs', bright, welcoming establishments, designed for a respectable middle-class clientele and elaborately furnished with carved woodwork, etched glass, mirrors and decorative tiles.

The Café Royal occupies a building dating from 1861, but owes its present appearance to major alterations made in the late 1890s. From its marble floor to its gilt plasterwork ceiling, supported by an elegant cast iron pillar with palm leaf capital, the interior of the Circle Bar is pure grandeur. In the centre is a majestic island counter – a distinctive feature of many Scottish bars of the late 19th century, designed to enable supervision of the customers. This public bar is separated by a carved walnut screen from the even more opulent Oyster Bar restaurant, where diners can still sup on these succulent bivalves – a long-standing staple of city taverns – at the marble-topped counter.

The walls of both bar and restaurant are adorned with splendid figurative panels of Doulton tiles, depicting famous inventors and great ships. The Oyster Bar, which has fine stained glass windows portraying Victorian sporting heroes, featured in the 1981 Oscar-winning film *Chariots of Fire*, the story of three British athletes at the 1924 Olympics.

Address 19 West Register Street, EH2 2AA, +44 (0)131 556 1884, www.caferoyaledinburgh.com | Getting there Lothian Buses 1, 4, 15, 16, 25, X26, 34 or X44 to Princes Street (Waverley Steps); Tram to St Andrew Square | Hours Sun–Wed 11am–11pm, Thu 11am–midnight, Fri & Sat 11am–1am | Tip Bennet's Bar at 8 Leven Street (next to the King's Theatre) is another city centre pub with a fine late Victorian interior, as well as good beer and whiskies.

10_The Caiystane

Strange sentinel in the suburbs

Though now incongruously set into a neat municipal alcove in a leafy suburban street, this colossal chunk of red sandstone has an arresting dignity that immediately casts the onlooker back to a very different era. To understand something of its significance, you have to allow your mind to clear away all the tidy gardens, houses and pavements and imagine it standing in open moorland, commanding sweeping views to the west and north, across the thickly wooded land to the hills and sea beyond.

The Caiystane is thought to have been erected around 5,000 years ago, in the period known as the Neolithic. It probably stood alone, and must have indicated that the site had some special significance. Several monuments and burials dated to the Bronze Age, up to 2,000 years later, have been unearthed nearby, all of which shows that the area was long held sacred to ancient people. Six of the mysterious hollows known as cup marks are carved into the rear of the stone, suggesting that the Caiystane itself was sacred too.

Standing nearly three metres high, the stone is oriented almost directly to the east and west. In ancient times, people read living features into the land around them, and it could be that they saw this wide boulder with flat sides as an immense hand, its narrow wrist emerging from the ground, with a thumb-like protrusion suggesting that its back faced west and its palm east. There are even striations at the top that could suggest fingers. Perhaps this giant's hand was erected to celebrate the sun's birth at dawn, its death at nightfall, and its highpoint at midday, when the shadow of the stone would have pointed due north.

We will never know for certain what our ancestors were thinking about when they set this massive stone in the earth, but its survival, even in such an unlikely context, provides an exciting springboard for speculation.

Address Caiystane View, EH10 6SQ | **Getting there** Lothian Buses 4 or 400 to Oxgangs Road (Caiystane View) | **Tip** A smaller standing stone, the Buckstane, can be seen about half a mile north on Braid Road, near the entrance to Mortonhall Golf Club. It's said to mark the place where the hounds were unleashed when medieval Scottish kings went hunting deer on the Boroughmuir.

11 The Caley Station Gates

Regal relic of the war of the railways

On a quiet west end side street, an ornate cast-iron gateway marks the entrance to what is now nothing more interesting than a hotel car park. This is a tiny remnant of the grand Victorian architecture of the long-gone 'Caley' – officially called Princes Street Station – terminal of the Caledonian Railway, which once occupied a huge area of land to the west of Lothian Road. For many decades, royalty and heads of state passed through its portals as they began official visits: the street-level station was always preferred to Waverley, at the other end of Princes Street, whose rather precipitous access made a dignified progress more awkward.

From the middle of the 19th century until early in the 20th, two major companies fought to dominate Scotland's booming rail system. Waverley Station was the terminus of the Caledonian's great rival, the North British Railway Company, which in 1846 opened the first track linking Edinburgh with the east coast of England. The previous year the Caledonian company had started work on a route from Glasgow to Carlisle, and in 1848 this was extended with a line to Edinburgh. Its initial terminal on Lothian Road expanded over the decades towards Princes Street, and in the 1890s it became the largest station in Scotland, with a 260-metre-long roof and grand classical façade. In 1895 the North British Company raised the stakes by beginning work on a luxury hotel at Waverley – the landmark now known as the Balmoral. Not to be outdone, the Caledonian line responded in 1904 with its own station hotel, a massive, grandiose red sandstone affair at the west end, which still looks as though it would be more at home in Glasgow.

The Caley station finally closed in 1965, but the hotel, recently reborn as the Waldorf Astoria, preserves both its gateway – now restored in its original colours – and another important relic: the station clock, still set five minutes fast as an aid to tardy travellers.

Address Rutland Street, EH1 2AN | **Getting there** Lothian Buses 3, 4, 25, 26, X26, 31, X31, 33, 44 or 100 to Shandwick Place; the gateway is to the south-west of the hotel building | **Tip** The far west end of Princes Street is known to locals as Binn's Corner, after the department store that once occupied the site. It became a popular meeting place, particularly for courting couples, after a delightful musical clock was installed there in 1960. Now restored by the building's new occupants, the Johnnie Walker Experience, it features a parade of kilted Highland pipers who circle the timepiece at 7 and 37 minutes past the hour, to the strains of *Scotland the Brave* and *Caller Herrin'*.

12 The Camera Obscura

Through a glass, darkly

Near the top of the steep incline of Castlehill stands a battlemented tower, capped by a white octagonal turret with a curious dome – the home of the Camera Obscura. This Latin term simply means 'dark room', and that's just what you find when you enter the rooftop gazebo. But then, as you watch bright moving pictures of the city's streets appear on the table-top in front of you, you realise that you are in fact standing inside a giant prototype of the photographic camera, which is in itself quite a thrill.

The Camera Obscura has been entertaining the Edinburgh public since 1853. It was the brainchild of a remarkable entrepreneur, Maria Theresa Short, who in 1835 set up her first visitor attraction, an observatory on Calton Hill. When that was closed down, she installed her telescope in the 17th-century tenement on Castlehill, adding a new floor to accommodate the original Camera Obscura – only the second of its kind in the world. It was taken over in 1892 by the urban reformer Patrick Geddes, who attempted for several decades to establish a 'sociological laboratory' in what he renamed the Outlook Tower. Now it has returned to being a popular science centre, with six floors displaying fascinating and sometimes alarming optical illusions, leading to the gentler sensation of the Camera Obscura at the very top.

The device is basically a development of the pinhole camera, which has been known for millennia. Using nothing more high-tech than a mirror, a series of lenses, and natural light, it projects an image through a small aperture at the top of the dome onto the large round screen below. The mirror can be rotated, to show real-time action from far and near – clouds scudding over the Pentlands, trams patrolling Princes Street, tourists converging on the castle. Even for denizens of an era jaded by imagery overkill, witnessing this soundless spectacle is a mysterious and magical experience.

Address Camera Obscura and World of Illusions, Castlehill, EH1 2ND, +44 (0)131 226 3709, www.camera-obscura.co.uk | **Getting there** Lothian Buses 9, 23 or 27 to George IV Bridge, then walk up Lawnmarket | **Hours** Daily, early–late. Check website for full details | **Tip** In a historic building a little further up Castlehill, the Contini Cannonball Restaurant serves imaginative Scottish food with an Italian twist, in stylish surroundings with splendid views. Its name comes from the cannonball lodged in the west wall, placed there centuries ago to mark the height of the piped water supply that once fed the Castlehill reservoir opposite (www.contini.com).

13_Cammo Park

Wild domain of the Black Widow

Once a magnificent country estate, now an enchanted wilderness, Cammo is one of the largest yet least visited public parks in Edinburgh. You sense its past grandeur as soon as you enter. Impressive avenues of trees flank a huge acreage of grassland, formerly an immaculate green, but now a meadow knee-deep in wild flowers. Soon the path leads you into tangled woods growing through the remains of an immense stable block, one of the few buildings still standing, ghostlike among the trees. Then the wood opens onto the heartland of the old garden, where the lawns are still mown, at the head of a handsome recreational canal. Here, on a grassy knoll, are the sad remains of the 17th-century Cammo House, long one of the most celebrated homes in Scotland, demolished in the 1980s after it fell into irreparable disrepair.

The park was originally the pride and joy of the visionary landowner Sir John Clerk of Penicuik. From 1710 onwards he planted specimen trees from around the world, including Britain's first monkey puzzle, established wind shelterbelts for exotic flower gardens and, most radically of all for his time, used poorer soil to create wilderness gardens as habitats for wildlife. The estate was maintained in all its splendour by a sequence of owners until the mid-20th century, when the cash-strapped dowager of the Maitland-Tennant family allowed it to become increasingly dilapidated and overgrown. Her infrequent sorties outside the gates, seated in sombre dress in the back of a black, curtained limousine, earned her the nickname of the Black Widow of Cammo. Her son Percival, who died in 1975, was finally reduced to living in a caravan, while his many dogs had the run of the crumbling house. Cammo is now run by the city council, who have extended Sir John's innovative wilderness policy to the whole park and turned it into one of the richest nature reserves in the city.

Address Cammo Road, EH4 8AW | **Getting there** Lothian Buses 43 to Queensferry Road (Braehead Avenue) and 0.5 mile walk, or Stagecoach X54, X55, X56, X59 or X60 to Barnton Junction and 0.8 mile walk | **Hours** Always open | **Tip** The Friends of Cammo community group undertake valuable work on the estate including tree planting and litter pick-ups. They also run a small visitor centre (with toilets) in the 18th-century Cammo Lodge, open Sun 2–4pm (www.friendsofcammo.org).

14_Castle Terrace Farmers' Market

From the field to the fork

The traditional open-air markets of Edinburgh disappeared over a century ago, though mementoes remain, in street names like Old Fishmarket Close and more tangible relics such as the Stockbridge Market archway. The occasional greengrocer's barrow lingered on, but for most of the 20th century nearly all food retailing in the city went on indoors, behind closed shop windows.

The concept of farmers' markets started in the USA, and was tried out in the UK for the first time in 1997. The idea that small-scale producers could get together to sell the fruits of their labours directly to local consumers, cutting out the middlemen, quickly caught on, and Edinburgh's new market traders first set out their stalls in Castle Terrace in June 2000. There are now over 50 regular farmers' markets across Scotland, but the Edinburgh exemplar, held on a tree-lined site on the south side of the castle rock, is the largest, and arguably the best. Since August 2020 it has been run as a stallholders' co-operative.

Every Saturday morning, whatever the weather, producers from throughout central and southern Scotland gather to sell a wide variety of seasonal fare. Locally reared meat, poultry, seasonal wild game and charcuterie are all strong features, and there's always a good range of fish and seafood, fresh and smoked, from both east and west coasts. Dairy produce is available from several makers – fine farmhouse cheeses of all kinds as well as fresh milk and butter. Organic produce stalls abound with delicious vegetables, freshly picked and dug, that come as a revelation to taste-buds blunted by their air-freighted supermarket equivalents. Soft fruit, a Scottish speciality, comes into its own in the summer, and artisan bread and preserves are on sale all year round. There's also a tasty selection of street food, coffee and tea – and don't miss the excellent craft beers, gins and liqueurs.

Address Castle Terrace, EH1 2EN, www.edinburghfarmersmarket.co.uk | **Getting there** Lothian Buses 1, 10, 11, 12, 15, 16, 24 or 47 to Lothian Road (Usher Hall), then walk down Cambridge Street | **Hours** Sat 9am–2pm | **Tip** Across the road from the market at 10 Cambridge Street is the Traverse Theatre, an Edinburgh legend dedicated to performing new writing. Founded in 1963, it moved to its present, purpose-built home in 1992, and has two auditoria plus an airy café-bar (www.traverse.co.uk).

15 The Catherine Sinclair Memorial

A philanthropic friend to children and animals

Famous men abound on the monuments of Edinburgh, mostly dedicated to forgotten politicians, aristocrats, and soldiers. But apart from the obligatory statue of Queen Victoria (at the foot of Leith Walk) the city has only one large-scale public memorial devoted to a woman: the once celebrated writer and philanthropist Catherine Sinclair (1800–64). Her neo-Gothic cenotaph, tall and stately like the lady herself, looks at first sight like a stray pinnacle from the Scott Monument, blown westwards by the fierce east wind. In fact it was inspired, appropriately, by the medieval Eleanor Crosses, erected by Edward I of England in memory of his intellectual and charitable queen.

Catherine Sinclair was a prolific writer of novels and travel guides, but her literary fame is chiefly due to her children's fiction. Her most famous work, *Holiday House* (1839), follows the sometimes mischievous exploits of young Laura and Harry Graham, including a boisterous picnic on Arthur's Seat. It was the first book in English to take a non-moralising attitude to children's misbehaviour, and was hugely popular, remaining in print for a century.

Another monument that used to bear her name was the large public drinking fountain she funded, the first in the city, which stood until 1932 at the west end of Princes Street, despite becoming an obstruction to traffic. It was for horses and dogs as well as people; an inscription on it read: 'Water is not for man alone.' She devoted much of her time to other charitable work for the ordinary folk of Edinburgh, instituting workers' canteens, founding a Boys' Brigade, and providing the first public benches on the city's thoroughfares.

Her memorial stands unobtrusively in a corner of the New Town, just down the hill from where she grew up, in Charlotte Square, a site that would later host Edinburgh's annual Book Festival.

Address North Charlotte Street (at the corner of Saint Colme Street), EH2 4HR | **Getting there** Lothian Buses 19, 22, 36, 37, 43, 47, 47B or 113 to Queensferry Street | **Tip** Several large carved and inscribed stones from the Sinclair Memorial Fountain are now located on the Water of Leith walkway and cycle path at Stedfastgate, by Gosford Place, Bonnington.

16 Chalmers Memorial Church

For those in peril on the sea

Fishing and mining have always been two of the most dangerous ways of gaining a livelihood, and as a result both activities have given rise to many devoutly religious communities. The Chalmers Memorial Church in the coastal village of Port Seton, just beyond the eastern edge of Edinburgh, was built to serve both the local fisherfolk and families at the nearby collieries. Imagery of the sea dominates the design of the church, not only because of the Christian symbolism of the fish, but also because fishing was by far the older industry, and the wealth it generated remained in the hands of local families. It was largely this congregation who paid for the church in 1904, and who decided on the Arts and Crafts style design by architect Sydney Mitchell, when a new building was needed to accommodate the rapidly expanding local mining communities.

The first impression you have on entering this uniquely delightful interior is of walking into, or rather under, a large upturned boat. The light floods in on all sides, but looking up into the arching roof all you see are rippling blue and white shadows. It's as if you're at sea, with the world turned upside down, the sky below you and the sea above, contained within the shape of a hull. This mesmeric effect, which is at once uplifting and soothing, has been artfully created not just by the rising rafters but, above all, by the blue and white stencilled decoration that seems to cover every surface with rolling waves, leaping fish and gulls in flight.

An informative free leaflet explains the history of the church and the symbolism that guided the design. Don't miss the little wood carving at the steps leading into the pulpit showing the fishermen who, obeying Jesus' instruction to fish on the other side of the boat, have hauled in a huge catch. It's an exquisite expression of faith and experience.

Address Gosford Road, Port Seton, Prestonpans, EH32 0HG, +44 (0)1875 812 225, www.chalmerschurch.co.uk | Getting there Lothian Buses 26 to Gosford Road (Inglis Avenue) | Hours Open for services Sun 11am. Guided tours are normally available in June/July, and the church is also a venue each September for world-class classical concerts during the Lammermuir Festival. | Tip It's a short walk from the church to the attractive 17th-century Port Seton harbour, which provided inspiration for much of the work of celebrated local artist, the late John Bellany.

17 The Church Hill Theatre

Much-loved temple of the performing arts

Morningside has had a lengthy association with religion. Place names like Canaan and Jordan Lane originated in the 17th century, when the area was rough country that provided refuge for outlawed Covenanters. Much later, as it grew into a douce Victorian suburb, pious churchgoers were spoilt for choice, with places of worship representing every denomination; on the northern fringe alone, four diverse establishments jostled for attention at the road junction that came to be dubbed Holy Corner. And it's just a short walk from there, up the rise called (inevitably) Church Hill, to yet another: an imposing red sandstone edifice built in 1892 as the home of Morningside Free Church.

The architect was the accomplished and prolific Hippolyte Blanc. His preferred mode for ecclesiastical work was neo-Gothic, but at the request of his clients he designed the Church Hill building in a plainer Renaissance Revival style. This proved an advantage after dwindling congregations led to the church's closure in the early 1960s. The enterprising town council of the day were keen to found a new 'centre for the arts, ballet, music and opera' for the use of local amateur groups, and they soon saw its potential for conversion into a proscenium-arched performance space.

The new Church Hill Theatre opened in September 1965 with a production by the Scottish Community Drama Association of Oscar Wilde's *The Importance of being Earnest* (written the year the church was completed) and that December Edinburgh People's Theatre began an annual tradition when they staged a lavish pantomime, *The Enchanted Waltz*. Over the decades since those heady days the Church Hill has become established as a favourite venue for a huge variety of local companies, generations of talented performers and appreciative audiences, and a recent refurbishment has ensured that it will go on serving its mission for decades to come.

Address Morningside Road, EH10 4DR, +44 (0)131 220 4348, www.churchhilltheatre.co.uk | Getting there Lothian Buses 11, 15, 16, 23 or 36 to Church Hill | Hours See website for programme. Bar opens 1 hour before shows | Tip A good choice for a pre-theatre meal is Tempo Perso, an authentic Italian restaurant less than five minutes' walk away at 206 Bruntsfield Place, EH10 4DE. Or if you've got a taste for exploring the former churches of Morningside, try Pizza Express at 1 Nile Grove, EH10 4RE, originally built in 1886 as Braid Church.

18 Craiglockhart War Hospital

Shellshocked in Dottyville

'There is nothing very attractive about the place.' This was Wilfred Owen's terse opinion of Craiglockhart War Hospital on his arrival there in June 1917, recorded in a letter to his mother. Despite its rural surroundings, the vast, sombre block of the former hydropathic institute must have seemed coldly clinical to the young soldier and poet, sent there to recover from the psychological trauma he was suffering after months of horrific trench warfare. However, his stay was to be a transformative episode in his tragically brief life: it was here that the subject of his poetry first became 'the pity of war'.

Craiglockhart was one of several hospitals set up during World War I to treat the huge number of soldiers severely traumatised by shellshock, with the aim of returning them to active duty. As part of the innovative therapy prescribed by his doctor, Arthur Brock, Owen was encouraged to write about his experiences, and to edit the hospital magazine, *The Hydra*, which included vivid poetry by patients unused to writing. Owen's other great influence at Craiglockhart was the older, published poet Siegfried Sassoon – a war hero, decorated for bravery, who was sent there for treatment after making a public stance criticising the conduct of the war. Rather than court-martial him, the authorities were persuaded to declare him mentally ill. With wry humour, Sassoon nicknamed the place 'Dottyville'. The intense relationship that he and Owen forged in their months there inspired some of the finest poetry to come out of the war.

Now part of Napier University, the building houses a small but poignant exhibition of material from their War Poets Collection. Owen returned to the front, and was killed just a week before the armistice; the display includes a photograph of the gloomy spot where he died. There was nothing very attractive about that place, either.

Address Craiglockhart Campus Library, Edinburgh Napier University, 219 Colinton Road, EH14 1DJ, +44 (0)131 455 3600, www.napier.ac.uk. The War Poets exhibition is in the building's original entrance hall. | **Getting there** Lothian Buses 4, 10, 27 or 45 to Colinton Road (Craiglockhart Campus), or 36 to the campus itself | **Hours** Daily 9am–5pm (may vary during university vacations and on public holidays – check website); email heritage@napier.co.uk beforehand to arrange a self-guided visit | **Tip** A War Poets Trail on the wooded Craiglockhart Hill follows paths that the soldiers would have taken; see www.eastercraiglockharthill.org for details and map.

19 Craigmillar Castle

This castle hath a pleasant seat

Every year, nearly two million visitors throng the battlements and halls of Edinburgh's most famous castle, but only a few thousand make it to its much more atmospheric cousin at Craigmillar, just three miles to the south east. In spite of the encircling housing schemes, Craigmillar Castle is still in a surprisingly rural setting, and it would be worth a visit for its location alone. But it's the fact that you can explore, virtually undisturbed, what is the most complete surviving medieval castle in Scotland that makes the experience particularly evocative and memorable.

As you listen to the calls of rooks and feel the wind on your face, it's easy to imagine what life was once like here – the cries of workers in the kitchens and gardens, the lords and ladies listening to music or dining in the halls, practising archery and hawking in the grounds. Soldiers patrolled the ramparts, alert for any intruders trying to scale the massive walls and ready to shoot them through the 'murder holes' in the stone flags under their feet.

Though it has long stood empty and roofless, many of the castle's inner chambers are virtually intact, as are its spiral staircases, which give easy access to the overhanging battlements and the immense tower in its centre, still standing proudly after 600 years. On the grassland below you can make out the indented outline of a huge letter P. This was once a fish pond, created for the Preston family, lords of the castle in late medieval times and sympathetic to Mary, Queen of Scots, who sought refuge at Craigmillar on several occasions, along with her French retinue. The district has been known as Little France ever since.

The views from the top are magnificent, across the Firth of Forth to the east and the Pentland Hills to the south. On the northwestern horizon you can see Edinburgh Castle, and picture the noisy crowds jostling one another.

Address Craigmillar Castle Road, EH16 4SY, +44 (0)131 661 4445, www.historicenvironment.scot | **Getting there** Lothian Buses 24, 33, 38 or 49 to Old Dalkeith Road (Little France). The castle is half a mile's walk from there; see website for advice on routes | **Hours** Daily, Apr–Sept 9.30am–5.30pm, Oct–Mar 9.30am–4pm | **Tip** Less than a mile back into town, Prestonfield House Hotel, a lavishly furnished 17th-century country house in extensive grounds, is a memorable (though expensive) place to go for a special meal or luxurious afternoon tea.

20 Cramond

The ferryman and the lion

Despite the intermittent screams of planes descending to the nearby airport, the village of Cramond, where the River Almond meets the Forth, is today a generally tranquil suburb and base for pleasure sailing. Its picturesque whitewashed cottages, built in the 18th century for workers in the iron mills, give it a homogeneous old-world appearance, but in fact the settlement has a much more ancient and varied history.

In 2001 an archaeological dig on the ancient foreshore revealed evidence of an encampment dating from around 8,600 B.C. – by far the earliest human habitation site then known in Scotland. As well as stone tools, the finds included heaps of shells from toasted hazelnuts, which would have nicely complemented the seafood fished from the estuary by these hunter-gatherers.

The next well-documented chapter in Cramond's history comes many millennia later, at the time of the Roman occupation of southern Scotland. Excavations last century uncovered an extensive fort and well-preserved bathhouse dating from around A.D. 140, which showed that Cramond was a major base and supply port for the forces who defended the Antonine Wall – the northernmost frontier of the Roman empire. Some of the remains can be seen on land near the church, though sadly the bathhouse is currently covered up.

But it was in the waters of the Almond estuary that Cramond's most striking ancient relic was found. In 1996, the boatman who rowed the now defunct passenger ferry (then the shortest crossing in the UK) spotted a curious stone sticking out of the mud, which turned out to be a 1.5-metre-long carving of a lioness devouring a man. Probably created for a Roman military tomb, the splendidly gory sculpture is now in the National Museum. The hapless victim is evidently a captive 'barbarian', and it's presumed that the monument was erected partly to act as a graphic warning to restless natives.

Address Cramond Village, EH4 6NU | Getting there Lothian Buses 47 to Cramond Green, then walk down Cramond Glebe Road | Tip There are noticeboards at key locations in the village with information about the Roman site. Don't miss lovely Cramond Kirk, rebuilt in 1656 over part of the fort; the interior is lined with splendid woodwork, and the kirkyard has some wonderful old gravestones.

21 Cramond Island

A haven and a barricade

Technically you're still in Edinburgh, but when you're walking on Cramond Island the apparent remoteness can be quite bewildering. Nevertheless, you have to keep reminding yourself that you can easily become genuinely cut off, for the causeway across Drum Sands that links it to the mainland is completely submerged at every high tide. A noticeboard on the foreshore gives visitors the safe crossing times.

This tidal island, almost a mile out into the Firth of Forth, is only a third of a mile long, and a little less in width, but it feels larger. Located opposite the mouth of the River Almond – known to have been inhabited in very ancient times – it was probably first used as a safe haven and a base for fishing, and at least one prehistoric burial has been unearthed there. The Romans built their most important harbour in Scotland on the Almond estuary, and must surely have occupied the island, probably exploiting its oyster beds, which were famous by the Middle Ages. In later centuries it was used for sheep rearing, and the ruins of an old farmhouse can still be seen in the woods. The last resident farmer died in 1904.

The 20th century brought development of a totally different type and scale. During World War I, the northern end was taken over for defensive purposes, and on the outbreak of World War II the whole island was requisitioned. Evocative ruins of gun emplacements, searchlight bases, storerooms, and winding gear for an anti-submarine net still litter the downriver side. The startling concrete pylons that flank the causeway are part of these defences, to stop submarines slipping past the landside of the island when the tide was high. But these wartime remnants don't detract from the essential peace and wildness of the place. Wandering along its secluded beaches, you feel as far from the concerns of the modern world as you could possibly be.

Address Opposite Cramond Village, EH4 6NU | **Getting there** Lothian Buses 47 to Cramond Glebe Road | **Hours** See notices displayed on the shore near the causeway for tide tables and information on safe crossing times, or text the word CRAMOND to 81400 | **Tip** Back on the mainland, the Boardwalk Beach Club is a relaxed and informal café on the coastal promenade, with a large outdoor seating area and a lovely outlook towards the island (50 Marine Drive, EH4 5ES, www.facebook.com/BoardwalkBeachClub).

22 Dean Bridge

A colossal masterwork

Owing to its exceptionally uneven topography, Edinburgh has 532 bridges within the boundaries – at least a hundred more than there are in Venice. Many of these are so integrated into the city-scape that they can hardly be seen: the long thoroughfare of South Bridge, for instance, is built on 29 spans, only one of which – the arch crossing the Cowgate – is actually visible.

But the most dramatic of the city's viaducts is surely the 32-metre-high Dean Bridge, which spans the deep gorge of the Water of Leith, carrying the main road leading from the West End to the northwestern suburbs. Completed in 1831, it was the last masterpiece of the renowned engineer Thomas Telford, the largely self-taught shepherd's son from Dumfriesshire who came to be nicknamed 'the Colossus of Roads'. Telford virtually invented the profession of civil engineering, and was responsible for thousands of superbly innovative bridges, canals, harbours, and roads that changed the face of Scotland and many other parts of Britain.

The design of the Dean Bridge combines far-sighted technical ingenuity with soaring elegance. Its massive piers are hollow, which reduced both their weight and their cost, but they've proved remarkably strong and stable, and more than capable of carrying volumes of traffic unimaginable in Telford's time, including abnormal load vehicles in excess of 150 tonnes. It's safe to assume that most of the thousands of motorists who use it every day are quite oblivious to the majesty of the four masonry arches beneath, which can best be appreciated from down in the lovely wooded ravine. When it was newly completed, the builder charged a penny to set foot on the bridge, so keen were the public to look out at its spectacular vistas. Sadly, suicide jumps later became so common that it was dubbed the 'Bridge of Sighs', and the parapet height had to be raised as a deterrent.

Address Queensferry Road, EH3 7UA | Getting there Lothian Buses 19, 22, 36, 37, 43, 47 or 113 to Queensferry Street; walk down Bell's Brae, then turn right into Miller Row to view the bridge from below | Tip Another impressive Telford viaduct is Lothian Bridge, which carries the A68 over the Tyne Water at Pathhead, 11 miles south of Edinburgh. Essentially a smaller version of the Dean Bridge, it's easier to see as a whole.

23 Dean Cemetery

A fashionable spot to rest undisturbed

Final resting places are thought of as hallowed and timeless, but in fact not many graveyards in Britain have been preserved undisturbed, or as they were originally laid out, and of these hardly any are still in use. The Dean Cemetery is a rare exception. Designed in 1845, and still run by the same organisation, it has burial plots available to this day. All that has really changed is that its landscaped grounds have gracefully matured. Trees planted as saplings over a century and a half ago now tower above the monuments, dappling them in sunlight and shade with their vast, spreading branches – the living embodiment of passing time.

When the Dean first opened its gates, Edinburgh was still haunted by memories of the 'resurrectionists', notorious since the 17th century for stealing corpses for surgical dissection from the gloomy, congested graveyards of the Old Town. The site of the new cemetery, to the west of the New Town on a high, green bank above the Water of Leith, was both secluded and secure. The land had formerly been the pleasure garden of a mansion house, and the cemetery design incorporated its high boundary walls and picturesque pathways.

The Dean quickly began to fill up with memorials to the great and the good of the day. William Playfair, the architect responsible for many of the city's iconic buildings, was buried here in 1857. Fine Victorian monuments abound to lawyers, authors, soldiers, scientists, and doctors, including Dr Joseph Bell, whose analytical mind inspired the character of Sherlock Holmes. Among many notable artists buried here are the bohemian Sam Bough, the fairy painter Joseph Noel Paton, and the pioneering photographer David Octavius Hill, who is commemorated in a bronze bust by his sculptor wife. Sadly, but fittingly, this coterie has recently been joined by the distinguished painter John Bellany, who died in 2013.

Address 63 Dean Path, EH4 3AT, +44 (0)131 332 1496, www.deancemetery.org.uk | **Getting there** Lothian Buses 19, 22, 36, 37, 43, 47 or 113 to Queensferry Road (Learmonth Terrace), then walk down Dean Path | **Hours** Daily: Apr–Sept 9am–5pm; Oct–Mar 9am–dusk | **Tip** Another atmospheric Victorian graveyard is Warriston Cemetery (42 Warriston Gardens, EH3 5NE). It boasts several notable graves including that of Sir James Young Simpson, pioneer of anaesthetics, and is gradually being restored thanks to an active Friends group.

24 Dean Village

Old mills by the stream

Just half a mile from the west end of Princes Street is a delightful surprise: a riverside village whose picturesque buildings are as unexpected as its rural seclusion. This charming, peaceful enclave is situated deep in the 'dene', or steep-sided valley, of the Water of Leith – once a much more powerful torrent than it is today. It was an ideal place for watermills, and grain was ground here from at least the 12th century.

By the 17th century the number of mills had grown to 11, and in 1675 the Incorporation of Baxters (bakers) built a fine granary, still standing in Bell's Brae, as their headquarters. A carved stone panel above the door shows the tools of their trade as well as the end product – three cakes and a pie. Despite the opening in 1832 of the Dean Bridge – effectively a high-rise bypass – the self-contained community continued to thrive until the late 19th century, when huge steam-powered flourmills in the port of Leith began to destroy the traditional industry. Tanneries, blacksmiths, and a chemical works were set up on the riverside, and it soon declined into a grimy industrial backwater.

In the 1880s the plight of Dean Village attracted the attention of John R. Findlay, the philanthropic proprietor of *The Scotsman* newspaper, whose house in Rothesay Terrace overlooked the valley. He paid for the construction of Well Court, a complex of social housing arranged around a central courtyard, complete with community hall and a splendid clock tower. Designed by Sydney Mitchell, with whimsical decorative features inspired by medieval Scots architecture, it no doubt improved the living conditions of local workers, while also greatly enhancing the view from Findlay's windows. The village fell into decline again in the mid-20th century, but sensitive restoration in recent decades has regenerated it into a unique and desirable residential neighbourhood.

Address Dean Village, EH2 4PF | **Getting there** Lothian Buses 19, 22, 36, 37, 43, 47 or 113 to Queensferry Street; walk towards Dean Bridge, then turn left down Bell's Brae | **Tip** The city's principal venues for modern and contemporary art, the Scottish National Gallery of Modern Art and the Dean Gallery, are a short walk west of Dean Village along the Water of Leith Walkway (signposted). Both are set in extensive parkland, and have popular cafés.

25 The Debenhams Building

Political enemies united in temple of mammon

When the first New Town was designed, Princes Street was intended to be residential. But after the draining of the swamp on its south side to create ornamental gardens, the one-sided thoroughfare with its panoramic views soon became the city's showplace street of commerce, and by the end of the 19th century a diverse array of shops, hotels and gentlemen's clubs had been erected. In the 1960s, however, a radical proposal for the large-scale redevelopment of key areas of the city finally took hold, and the wrecker's ball began to destroy Princes Street's grand old buildings. The brutalist blocks that replaced them had to incorporate upper terraces, the intention being that the whole street would eventually be recast as a row of identikit modern buildings linked by a first-floor walkway.

By 1978, when Debenhams acquired the former Conservative Club building and the adjacent Liberal Club for their new flagship store, the city planners had, thankfully, lost their nerve, and this absurd ambition had been abandoned. The retail giant was obliged to conserve not only the palatial façades, but also major elements of both clubs' interiors. This resulted in the curious circumstance of two Victorian political giants and bitter rivals sharing space within a modern temple of mammon. An ornate processional staircase was relocated to the back of the store, along with a fine tripartite stained-glass window dedicated to Benjamin Disraeli, while a book-lined mahogany library, ornamented with a marble bust of William Gladstone, was incongruously repurposed as part of the ladies' clothing department.

But the inexorable decline of the traditional department store, precipitated by the Covid pandemic, led to Debenhams' permanent closure in 2021. After a period of uncertainty about the future of the unique historic building, it is now being converted into an upmarket hotel focussed on rest and well-being.

Address 109–112 Princes Street, EH2 3AA | **Getting there** Lothian Buses 1, 4, 15, 19, 26, 34, 44 or 113 to Princes Street West | **Hours** Currently viewable from outside only | **Tip** Behind the Debenhams building at 152–154 Rose Street is The Kenilworth, one of several traditional pubs in this pedestrianised lane. Named after a novel by Sir Walter Scott, it has a fine Victorian interior, a good range of ales and whiskies, and serves food all day.

26 The Dominion Cinema

Grand old lady of the silver screen

When the Dominion first opened for business in January 1938, it must have looked as though it had been shipped straight from Hollywood to Morningside. With a glamorous Streamline Moderne façade, deluxe interior fittings and the latest in projection and sound equipment, the 1,360-seat picture palace cost £25,000 to build, and was completed in just 16 weeks. It was an immediate success, and soon put paid to the nearby Springvalley Cinema, one of the 35 other picturehouses then operating in the city. Twenty-five years later, when cinemas all over the country were closing down as they lost out to the rival television, it was still entertaining a regular audience of 8,000 a week.

Always independent and run by the same family, the Dominion has survived triumphantly into the age of the multiplex, moving with the times without ever compromising the standards set by its founder, Captain W. M. Cameron. Right from the start his aim was to offer patrons a superior viewing experience, with 'maximum comfort and courtesy', as he announced on the opening night. Now run by the third generation of Camerons, the 'Dom', as it is familiarly known, continues to have a special place in the hearts of its local public. The Captain always refused to screen 'adult' films with an X rating, and his descendants proudly uphold the spirit of his policy, providing quality family entertainment in a friendly atmosphere.

The building has seen many internal alterations over the years as it has confronted the challenge of changing viewing habits, and it now boasts four screens, all furnished with exceptionally comfortable seating. Photos lining the stairs recall its long history, and portray some of the film stars welcomed over the decades by its late manager Derek Cameron, including the suave Cary Grant. Cameron later described him as 'charming' – adding wryly that the same could, of course, be said of all the other stars he'd ever met.

Address 18 Newbattle Terrace, EH10 4RT, +44 (0)131 447 4771, www.dominioncinema.co.uk | Getting there Lothian Buses 5, 11, 15, 16, 23 or 36 to Morningside Road (Church Hill) | Hours Daily; check website for showtimes | Tip A short way down the main street at 237 Morningside Road is The Canny Man's, a quirky old-established local with an impressive range of whiskies, each served with the appropriate spring water, and a menu based on Danish-style open sandwiches.

27_Dovecot Studios

Textiles that make a splash

The municipal baths in Infirmary Street were the first public swimming pool and bathhouse complex in Edinburgh. Opened in 1887, with a separate pool for ladies, they were in continuous use for just over a century before they fell into disrepair, and were closed in the 1990s. What had been a much-loved local facility rapidly became derelict, and the building was threatened with demolition before it was finally sold in 2006, to be converted into new premises for the tapestry-weaving company Dovecot Studios.

This company also has a long and venerable history. Established in 1912, in a purpose-built workshop in the west of Edinburgh (adjacent to an old pigeon house – hence the name), it was the creation of the fourth Marquess of Bute. Inspired by William Morris' tapestry workshop in London, he decided to set up a Scottish equivalent, originally to furnish his own residences. After World War II the studios developed into a commercial concern, and soon became internationally renowned for their interpretation of designs by leading artists of the day, including Stanley Spencer, Henry Moore, and David Hockney.

The Dovecot today has a team of six weavers working in the imaginatively converted pool. The main arcaded hall of cast-iron pillars, which formerly echoed to the splashing and shrieks of generations of swimmers, is now a hushed hive of industry, where these experts sit at vast looms, using traditional techniques to create innovative contemporary textiles. In the upper gallery, which used to house cubicles with baths, there is a viewing balcony where visitors can watch the work on the weaving floor, and also see displays of the finished products. Other rooms in the complex have been converted into spacious galleries, with a programme of exhibitions on art, craft and design themes; there are regular hands-on workshops and other events, plus a well-stocked shop and a popular café.

Address 10 Infirmary Street, EH1 1LT, +44 (0)131 550 3660, www.dovecotstudios.com | Getting there Lothian Buses 3, 5, 7, 8, 14, 29, X29, 30, 31, 33, X33, 35, 37, 45 or 49 to South Bridge | Hours Mon–Sat 10am–5pm; Viewing Balcony: Mon–Fri noon–3pm, Sat 10am–5pm | Tip The beehive-shaped 16th-century Corstorphine Dovecot, which gave its name to the original studios, is in a good state of preservation, and well worth a look (Dovecot Road, EH12 7LE).

28 Dr Neil's Garden

Horticultural healing

Edinburgh has a surprising number of secret gardens, hidden down Old Town closes and behind New Town railings, but perhaps the most unexpectedly special is a secluded retreat, open to all, in the waterside village of Duddingston, just a couple of miles from the city centre. Though the main street of this picturesque former weaving settlement is now blighted by constant traffic, the verdant wooded terraces of the garden between the church and the loch remain a haven of tranquillity, seemingly far from the rat-run.

Strolling along the meandering paths, or sitting under the towering pines, all you hear is the breeze in the leaves around you and in the reeds that line the water's edge. Occasionally a duck squawks, a gull cries, or a heron flaps lazily over the loch. The planting is an exquisite marriage of nature and nurture: wild irises flourish with exotics, bluebells with azaleas.

This oasis of bliss was created by doctors Andrew and Nancy Neil, a husband and wife team who ran a general medical practice. In 1963 they began, in their spare time, to cultivate the stony, sloping field behind Duddingston Kirk, which had until then been used as grazing land for calves and geese. With years of painstaking effort, the Neils transformed the south-facing promontory into a magnificent landscaped garden. Many of the plants were collected by the energetic pair on their holidays caravanning on the continent. They encouraged some of their patients to join them in the healthy exercise of horticulture, and so the Neils' garden grew and thrived. It was always public in spirit, and in 1997 a charitable trust was formed to keep it so. The Neils both died in 2005, but the garden continues to be excellently maintained and developed by the trust. In 2013, a Physic Garden was created on the site to commemorate the lives, as both doctors and gardeners, of these remarkable Edinburgh benefactors.

Address Old Church Lane, EH15 3PX, +44 (0)7849 187 995, www.drneilsgarden.co.uk | **Getting there** Lothian Buses 12 to Duddingston Road West; the entrance to the garden is through the gates to Duddingston Manse, at the end of the path leading to the right | **Hours** Daily 10am–dusk | **Tip** The ancient, picturesque Duddingston Kirk has recently developed part of the adjacent glebe land as a community garden, growing organic produce while training volunteers from diverse backgrounds in horticultural skills (www.jocktamsonsgairden.org.uk). The church also has a Garden Room café (Easter–Sept, Thu & Fri 10am–4pm, Sat & Sun 1–4pm). Look out for the 19th-century watchtower in the kirkyard, built to deter body snatchers.

29 Dreaming Spires

Walking tall outside the multiplex

You don't expect to come across a pair of giraffes on an Edinburgh pavement, particularly not at the top of Leith Walk, the wide, windswept thoroughfare that leads down to the old port. In recent decades, city planners dreamed of turning it into a continental boulevard, ignoring the absence of constant sunshine and chic pavement cafés. They thought that sculpture would help to create a sophisticated ambience, and a distinctly odd assembly of bronzes has now gathered here, including a flock of pigeons, a gigantic foot, and even Sherlock Holmes. (His creator, Arthur Conan Doyle, was born in nearby Picardy Place.)

By far the most successful are Helen Denerley's giraffes, which lift the gaze and the spirit beyond the concrete jungle. The artist had the idea when, in 2004, she entered the competition to create a sculpture outside the Omni Centre: an addition to Leith Walk's art parade was a condition of planning consent for this vast leisure complex. The footprint allotted for the artwork was disproportionately small – so Helen decided to go tall. She had already established an international career as an artist in scrap metal, working as far afield as Japan and South Georgia, recycling living creatures out of the very instruments of their destruction. And so she chose to create a mother and baby giraffe, their loving relationship vividly expressed in the curves of car bodies and motorcycle parts.

Strangely, these larger-than-lifesize creatures resonate with Edinburgh. They look towards the Old Town, long famous for its immensely tall buildings, where the gentry held their heads high, full of moral rectitude. Encircling them is a quotation set in bronze from Roy Campbell's poem 'Giraffes': 'a People who live between earth and skies / Each in his own religious steeple / Keeping a lighthouse with his eyes.' The official title of the work is *Dreaming Spires*, but Helen knows the pair as Martha and Gilbert.

Address Greenside Place, EH1 3AA | Getting there Lothian Buses 1, 4, 5, 7, 8, 14, 16, 19, 25, 29, 31, 34, 37, 45 or 49 to Leith Street; Tram to Picardy Place | Tip Edinburgh's original Italian deli, the legendary Valvona & Crolla, is a few minutes' walk down the road. It has a popular café-bar at the back of the shop – pricey, but excellent quality (www.valvonacrolla.co.uk).

30 Dreghorn Practice Trenches

Preparing for the hell of the Somme

A narrow, well-trodden path leads south from Redford Road to the east of Bonaly Burn. It climbs into a thick wood, then turns abruptly at a high fence capped with razor wire, the boundary of Dreghorn Barracks. As you continue along the path, there are glimpses, through the trees to the right, of the stream at the foot of the gorge, while on your left, beyond the wire mesh, you can see army buildings and soldiers going about their duties. This juxtaposition of nature and warfare is an apt prelude to the site that you soon come to, where trees have been cleared to reveal a configuration of ditches and dug-outs, some still banked with stones and rusting sheets of corrugated iron.

These are World War I practice trenches, dug by volunteer soldiers training in the techniques of fighting on the front line. Live ammunition would often have been used in the exercises, though even this could not have fully prepared the men for the horrors they were soon to face. The complex of trenches at Dreghorn were saved, and are now listed as a historic monument, thanks largely to the determined efforts of local historian Lynne Gladstone-Millar, whose father trained in them before the Battle of the Somme. He survived the Great War, and told her much later of his training experience, remembering especially the mud, which the men called 'Dreghorn Sludge'. It caked on to the pleats of their kilts, lacerating their legs like knives.

After Great Britain declared war on 4 August, 1914, tens of thousands of men responded to the call 'Your King and Country Need You', and went on to train in similar sites throughout the country. The fact that nature has done its best to reclaim the Dreghorn trenches, with a century's deposit of leaf mould, makes their impact particularly moving. The continuing reality of war today is brought home by the distant sound of firing from the barracks.

Address Redford Wood, Redford Road, EH13 9QJ | Getting there Lothian Buses 16 to Redford Road (Dreghorn Park); follow the path into the woodland by Bonaly Burn | Tip The Scottish National War Memorial, a shrine within the walls of Edinburgh Castle, was opened in 1927 to the memory of Scots who died in World War I. Though there is normally a hefty fee to enter the Castle, the Memorial can be visited free of charge, on application to the Castle Ticket Office (daily 9.30am–5pm or 6pm, depending on the season).

31 Dunbar's Close Garden

The spirit of gardens past

Fig trees, topiary, and the sweet smell of box hedges are sights and scents associated more with the environs of Florence than the centre of Edinburgh, but 350 years ago these were common features of the walled gardens that lay behind the townhouses flanking the Canongate. The street takes its name from the canons of Holyrood Abbey, whose *gait* (way) it once was; its proximity to the royal palace attracted the 17th-century nobility to build mansions on the spacious plots of what was then a separate burgh, outside the overcrowded city.

Formal terraced gardens in the continental style, with parterres and orchards, became *de rigueur* on the sloping land to the rear; a detailed city map of 1647 shows their great number and extent. These weren't solely ornamental pleasure grounds – vegetables, herbs, and fruit were also extensively cultivated. Moray House, on the sunny south side, was particularly famed for the produce from its fruit trees, which included figs and apricots.

Dunbar's Close Garden was created 50 years ago with the intention of recapturing the spirit of these long-gone Edens. The close, just beyond the south wall of Canongate Kirkyard, had once been home to Mrs Love's tavern, where in 1786 Robert Burns watched society ladies downing copious quantities of ale and oysters. But by the 1970s the area had become a neglected gap site. The Mushroom Trust charity bought the land and had it restored in the style of a 17th-century formal garden, using mainly historic plant varieties, though the decision was taken to omit vegetables.

The result is a little gem, with much to delight the horticultural enthusiast – wonderful displays of fritillaries in the spring and, a little later, exquisite Florentine irises. There's also a border of ancient roses, including *Rosa alba*, the white rose of the Jacobites. But it's an equally welcome find for the non-specialist visitor, in search of a peaceful and fragrant green corner in the city.

Address Dunbar's Close, 137 Canongate, EH8 8BW | Getting there Lothian Buses 35 to Canongate | Hours Daily from 7am; closing time varies with the season – check on www.edinburghoutdoors.org.uk or phone +44 (0)131 529 5151 | Tip Clarinda's Tearoom at 69 Canongate is a long-established traditional café, famed for its home baking (+44 (0)131 557 1888, Tue–Fri 10am–4.30pm, Sat & Sun 9.30am–4.30pm). The original Clarinda was a friend and muse of the poet Robert Burns; her grave is in nearby Canongate Kirkyard.

32 Dundas House Banking Hall

The star-spangled vault

Scotland rejoices in having three banks that each print their own notes – still a source of general pride, even in our increasingly cashless times. These have featured many memorable designs over the years, among them the concentric rings of stars that long served as a background on those of the Royal Bank, a stylish graphic based on the celestially domed ceiling that soars above the central hall of its magnificent headquarters.

The bank occupies what was formerly a grand townhouse, built in the early 1770s for the entrepreneur and local MP Sir Lawrence Dundas, a 'cunning shrewd man of the world' who deliberately subverted architect James Craig's original design for the New Town. Shortly before the town council finally approved the plans, which were to include a church dedicated to Andrew, Scotland's patron saint, on a large plot at the east end, Dundas acquired this prime site for his own home. The three-storey Palladian villa that he built there was described as 'incomparably handsome', but by the time of his death in 1781 the construction of the New Town had begun in earnest, and the surrounding area was a building site. Finding the house less agreeable, his son sold it to the government for use as offices. It was finally bought by the Royal Bank in 1825.

In 1859 they commissioned major reconstruction work to make the building even grander. Local architect J. Dick Peddie designed the new banking hall with a vast iron-framed dome springing from four ornate arches. The 120 stars that punctuate it are in fact glazed windows, arranged in five circles of diminishing size around a central sunburst oculus. It's both a breathtaking design concept and an ingenious lighting solution for what was (and still is) a working bank, as well as a sumptuous showplace.

Address Royal Bank of Scotland, 36 St Andrew Square, EH2 2AD | **Getting there** Lothian Buses 1, 4, 10, 11, 15, 16, 19 or 34 to Princes Street (Scott Monument), or Tram to St Andrew Square | **Hours** Mon–Sat; check opening times on +44 (0)3457 242424 | **Tip** Across the square at 14 George Street, there is another grand domed banking hall where you can have a meal or a drink – the former headquarters of the Commercial Bank of Scotland, now the award-winning Dome restaurant (www.thedomeedinburgh.com).

33 Edinburgh College of Art Sculpture Court

Casting around for classical perfection

The Trustees' Academy of Edinburgh, founded in 1760 to teach drawing, was the first public school of art in Britain. An essential part of an artist's training at the time was the study of classical sculpture. But even in the city that called itself the Athens of the North, ancient Greek prototypes were hard to come by, and so in 1798 the academy began to collect plaster casts of antique statues and carved reliefs.

Meanwhile, in Athens proper, Scottish diplomat Lord Elgin was on a mission to preserve the sculptures of the Parthenon, prime exemplars of the highest flowering of classical art, which were in a neglected and vulnerable state. He began by making casts, but soon proceeded with the wholesale removal from the temple of about half of the remaining sculptures, which he then transported to Britain. Their eventual acquisition in 1816 by the British Museum caused an artistic sensation – as well as a bitter controversy that reverberates to this day.

The Edinburgh Trustees were quick to obtain a cast of every one of the 'Elgin Marbles', taken from the first moulds to be made of the sculptures. This set the standard for their teaching collection, and they continued to seek out only the finest impressions available, acquiring some intended for the French Academy, and paying agents in Italy to make new moulds of Roman statues.

In the later 19th century the collection became a popular attraction for the Edinburgh public, and when the new College of Art was instituted in 1906, the casts were given to it on condition that they remained freely accessible to all. The College's two-tier, Beaux-Arts-style sculpture court was specially designed to display the entire Parthenon frieze around its walls, and more casts of fine quality, including ancient Greek and Italian Renaissance pieces, can be found under the arcades and dotted around nearby corridors.

Address Edinburgh College of Art, 74 Lauriston Place, EH3 9DF, +44 (0)131 651 5800, www.eca.ed.ac.uk | **Getting there** Lothian Buses 23, 27, 35, 45 or 47, or McGill's Bus 60 to Lauriston Place (Chalmers Street) | **Hours** Daily; phone or email eca@ed.ac.uk to check | **Tip** The Albacini collection of casts of Roman portrait busts, originally in the Trustees' Academy, is now in the National Gallery of Scotland on the Mound. The finest items are normally on display in the stairway leading to the upper floor, at the back of the main gallery building.

34 Edinburgh Printmakers

The freedom of the press

In April 2019, a long-established art workshop open to all comers entered an exciting new phase with the opening of its latest premises: a converted factory with 2,650 square meters of light-filled space, in an area undergoing regeneration. The long-abandoned brick building that is now the home of Edinburgh Printmakers is part of the 19th-century Castle Mills complex, formerly occupied by the North British Rubber Company (once the largest employer in the city), and later by Scottish and Newcastle breweries. The sensitive restoration incorporates many original features, plus specially commissioned artwork that reflects its industrial heritage, including charming panels featuring casts of products such as hot-water bottles.

Such creative repurposing of houses of drudgery is something of a habit for Edinburgh Printmakers – their previous home, for over 30 years, was an ex-public laundry. But in fact the history of this laudable enterprise goes back well over five decades. It was in the heady days of 1967 that they set up their original open access print studio, the first in the UK, next to a gallery in Victoria Street. Their formula of offering top-class facilities and technical support to professional artists as well as novices soon caught on, and during the 1970s it spawned similarly innovative and successful set-ups in Glasgow, Aberdeen and Dundee.

The new creative hub at Castle Mills is one of the largest facilities of its kind in Europe, with extensive printmaking studios and two galleries, as well as a shop selling prints and other handmade products, and a lovely café. It welcomes amateur enthusiasts and community groups as much as the many established artists who go there to practise their craft. The Printmakers' expert staff run courses at all levels, varying from taster sessions to summer schools, in a wide range of techniques, ancient and modern – relief printing, etching, lithography, screen-printing and digital processes.

Address 1 Dundee Street, EH3 9FP, +44 (0)131 557 2479, www.edinburghprintmakers.co.uk | **Getting there** Lothian Buses 1, 34 or 35 to Fountainbridge (Gilmore Park) | **Hours** Exhibitions and shop Wed–Sun 10am–6pm, café and studios Tue–Sat from 10am. See website for full details, and for information on courses and workshops. | **Tip** Edinburgh Quay, the terminus of the Union Canal, is just behind the Castle Mills building. Take a short stroll east along the towpath to see Shona Kinloch's striking bronze sculptural group of ten life-size swans.

35 Fettes College

OTT old school of 007

It's astonishing to learn that the palatial Fettes College, with its extravagant ornamentation of spires and turrets, and commanding setting in 100 acres of wooded parkland, was originally intended for the education of poor orphans and other disadvantaged children. That was the wish of William Fettes, a wealthy merchant, underwriter, and former Lord Provost, who in 1836 left a considerable endowment for its construction, and when it finally opened in 1870 its first intake of 53 pupils were indeed almost all orphan boys. However, the philanthropic aims of its founder no longer hold sway, and Fettes College is now one of Scotland's most exclusive private schools.

The monumental building that dominates the city's northern skyline is the work of David Bryce, the most prolific and versatile Scottish architect of the day. Bryce could turn his hand to virtually any style – Palladian, Gothic or Scottish Baronial. His inspiration for Fettes College came largely from a tour of northern France: the chateaux of the Loire Valley, particularly Chambord and Blois, were major influences on both layout and detailing, and he based the fantastical pinnacle of the skyscraping central tower on the belfry of the medieval town hall at Douai.

The school's former pupils include ex-prime minister Tony Blair and actress Tilda Swinton, but its most famous alumnus is the fictional character known the world over as agent 007. According to the backstory revealed in the final two novels by his creator Ian Fleming, James Bond was orphaned as a child of 11 – though he was hardly the sort of pupil that William Fettes had in mind. Expelled from Eton at the age of 13 after a liaison with a chambermaid, Bond was then sent to Fettes by his aunt Charmian. He excelled at sports, especially boxing, and founded the first judo class at a British school before leaving, aged just 17.

Address Carrington Road, EH4 1QX | Getting there Lothian Buses 24 or 29 to Comely Bank Road (Learmonth Grove); the school is at the end of Fettes Avenue | Hours Though it can be hired during school holidays for events such as weddings, Fettes is not otherwise open to the public. There's a good view of the exterior from the rooftop car park of the Waitrose supermarket at 38 Comely Bank Road. | Tip At the other end of the scale in architectural extravagance is the modestly austere classical building of Edinburgh Academy, another of the city's great schools, at 42 Henderson Row, EH3 5BL, in nearby Stockbridge.

36 The Flodden Tower

Keeping the English out

On 10 September, 1513, the town council of Edinburgh issued a proclamation commanding its citizens to prepare themselves for war. The previous day, the Scots army under James IV had gone into battle against the forces of Henry VIII, just over the border at Flodden Field. Early rumours of a disastrous defeat turned out to be all too true: King James himself had been killed, along with many thousands of men, including members of virtually every noble family in Scotland.

There was widespread fear that the English would soon march on Edinburgh, and the council took swift action to build defences. It was the southern and eastern boundaries that were most vulnerable to attack; the unassailable Castle Rock, and the marshy Nor' Loch (now Princes Street Gardens) protected the city to the north and west. From 1514, work began on the reinforcement of the existing town walls, erected by James II around the middle of the previous century, and on the construction of a lengthy extension, to enclose the fashionable southern suburbs of the Cowgate and Grassmarket. But the threatened attack never materialised, and it was not until 1560 that the Flodden Wall was completed. Similar delays have characterised many of the city's construction projects ever since.

Sections of the wall survive in several locations, but the most evocative remnant is this sturdy bastion at its south-west corner. Though rather truncated by the present-day road level, the battlemented Flodden Tower still has a formidable appearance. Looking at the inside of the walls, you can see how the gunloops were set into splayed openings, which gave the defender a wide field of fire while presenting a very narrow target.

The pinkish rubble for the tower came from the quarry at nearby Bruntsfield Links. The dark orange masonry of Telfer's Wall, built in 1620 to enclose a further 10 acres, extends to its south.

Address The Vennel, EH1 2HU; at the top of the steps | **Getting there** Lothian Buses 23, 27, 35, 45 or 47 to Lauriston Place, then walk down Heriot Place | **Tip** Another section of the Flodden Wall can be seen nearby at the west end of Greyfriars Kirkyard, and there is a longer stretch, lacking battlements, at the junction of Drummond Street and the Pleasance.

37_The Forth Bridge

Made in Scotland, from girders

There's only one Forth Bridge – the mighty wonder of the Victorian world that carries the railway across the firth at Queensferry. Other crossings do span the Forth, and the rail bridge now has two close companions to take the road traffic. But, fine feats of engineering though they no doubt are, neither the spanking new Queensferry Crossing nor the prematurely ageing Road Bridge can begin to compete with the majestic presence and iconic status of the original.

Comparisons have been made with the near-contemporary Eiffel Tower, and the Forth Bridge is clearly part of the same *zeitgeist*. Both are constructed from a complex network of latticed metal – wrought iron in the case of the tower, and for the bridge the novel medium of steel. But whereas the Eiffel Tower was only ever meant to be a temporary leisure attraction, the Forth Bridge had a serious purpose, and its design had to inspire total confidence in its durability and permanence.

There was a very good reason for this. In 1878 a two-mile long, 85-span bridge had been completed to take the railway over the River Tay, some 50 miles north. It was so admired that its designer was commissioned to build a similar crossing on the Forth. But in 1879 the Tay Bridge collapsed in a violent storm, taking with it a train carrying 75 passengers and crew. Plans for the Forth suspension bridge were abandoned, and in 1883 work began on a new, reassuringly massive structure based on three cantilevers resting on huge granite piers. Shortly before it opened in 1890, it was blasted by the fiercest gale hitherto recorded in the area, and shifted less than an inch.

Painting the bridge has gone down in legend and anecdote as a never-ending task, but a 10-year-long paint job was completed in 2011 that should dispel that myth and last for decades. The new hardy coating was specially mixed to match the original shade, known, naturally, as Forth Bridge Red.

Address Firth of Forth, between South Queensferry & North Queensferry | **Getting there** Lothian Buses (East Coast) 43 to South Queensferry, or train to Dalmeny, then follow footpath to South Queensferry – or continue by rail across the bridge itself to North Queensferry. Two companies operate cruises from South Queensferry that sail under the bridge: www.maidoftheforth.co.uk & www.forthtours.com | **Tip** Located under the north end, the Deep Sea World aquarium features a large collection of sharks and one of the world's longest underwater tunnels (Forthside Terrace, North Queensferry, KY11 1JR).

38 The French Institute

An old and cultured ally

In a speech made in Edinburgh in 1942, Charles de Gaulle, the leader of the Free French, referred to the friendship between his country and Scotland as 'the oldest alliance in the world'. It was a mutual distrust of England that had first formally united the two nations. In 1295, the Scots and French kings signed a pact committing them to support the other in the event of an attack on either by the English. The Auld Alliance, as it became known, was ratified by the monarchs of both countries up until 1568, and this close relationship has lingered on through the centuries in many aspects of Scottish life. Even the names of some quintessentially Scottish products are derived from French – haggis from *hachis*, meaning minced meat, and tartan from *tiretaine*, a woollen cloth.

Edinburgh's French Institute was set up in 1946 to maintain and build on this long-standing connection. It was the brainchild of Ambassador René Massigli, who had served alongside de Gaulle during World War II, and it is a product of his belief in maintaining peace by promoting cross-cultural exchange. The Institute is part of the French Foreign Ministry.

In addition to running language classes for all ages, the Institute has a media library and an all-day bistro. It hosts a lively year-round programme of talks, films, concerts, theatre and exhibitions, as well as co-operating in other cultural events with a French connection. Its regular tutored wine tastings are also deservedly popular in the city whose famed fondness for claret goes back to the Middle Ages.

After many decades based in a Georgian townhouse in the West End, the Institute has recently relocated, along with the French Consulate, to the heart of the Old Town. Its prestigious new home, opposite St Giles' Cathedral, is a grand neoclassical block built in 1905 for Midlothian County Council. The solemnly heroic frieze on the east façade depicts the industries of Mining, Agriculture and Fishing.

Address West Parliament Square, EH1 1EF, +44 (0)131 285 6030, www.ifecosse.org.uk | **Getting there** Lothian Buses 9, 23 or 27 to George IV Bridge | **Hours** Library Tue–Fri 9.30am–5pm, Sat 9.30am–1pm, bistro Sun–Thu 9am–9.30pm, Fri & Sat 9am–10pm. For films, events and courses see website. | **Tip** The main building of the National Library of Scotland is adjacent on George IV Bridge. It has a changing programme of free exhibitions based on books and documents from its vast collections, and also runs regular tours and workshops (www.nls.uk; exhibitions: Mon–Thu 10am–7pm, Fri & Sat 10am–5pm).

39 General Register House Rotunda

A Pantheon for the nation's archives

The home of the nation's public records, designed in 1771 by Scottish architect Robert Adam, is one of the city's very finest buildings. Sadly, the visual impact it once had, standing on a long landscaped terrace at the foot of North Bridge, has been greatly reduced and eroded by subsequent development and road widening, not to mention the ungainly equestrian statue of Wellington rearing in front of it, and General Register House is now little regarded by passers-by.

The interior, however, has fared much better, and even if you're not interested in tracing your Scots ancestry, it's well worth entering the building just to gaze at its central room, a rotunda inspired by the Roman Pantheon. It's a marvellous concept: a vast drum lined with book-filled arcades, crowned with a 24-metre-high dome embellished with elegant neoclassical plasterwork – Adam's trademark – which includes a discreet Scottish thistle motif.

After the Act of Union in 1707, the Scots were determined that their national archives should be kept in Edinburgh. It took a long time to raise sufficient funds for an appropriate new building, and it was 1774 before work finally began. Robert Adam was an ideal choice for the project of creating Britain's first custom-built record repository, using his knowledge of Roman architecture in incorporating underfloor heating to dispel damp, as well as in the solid stone construction, to reduce the risk of fire. In 1779, rising costs led to the suspension of building work, and for six years the rotunda lay roofless. It had a startling moment of fame when the eccentric James Tytler inflated his 12-metre hot-air balloon – later to make the first manned ascent from British soil – inside its walls. Finally completed in 1789 and largely unchanged today, it is a uniquely agreeable place for Scots and their visiting diaspora to research family history.

Address 2 Princes Street, EH1 3YY, +44 (0)131 535 1314, www.nrscotland.gov.uk | **Getting there** Lothian Buses 1, 4, 15, 16, 19, 25, 26, X26, 29, 34, 37, 44 or X44 to Princes Street (Waverley Steps) | **Hours** Mon–Fri 9am–4.30pm | **Tip** Cross the road to the Balmoral Hotel and treat yourself to a sumptuous afternoon tea under the glass dome of its Palm Court – expensive but memorable (daily noon–5pm; phone +44 (0)131 556 2414 to book).

40 George Heriot's School

The great soul of Jingling Geordie

When King James VI left Scotland in 1603 to assume the throne of England, royal goldsmith George Heriot closed his booth at St Giles and followed the court to London. Heriot's business, which included lending money – at 10 per cent interest – to the spendthrift monarch, as well as supplying jewellery to his extravagant queen, had already made him one of the wealthiest men in Scotland. It was supposedly the sound of all the coins clinking in his purse that led to his nickname of 'Jingling Geordie'. He spent the rest of his life in London, and continued to prosper. But when he died in 1624, without legitimate heirs, it was to his native city that he left his considerable fortune, directing the town council to spend it on endowing a charity school for 'fatherless bairns'.

A site was acquired on High Riggs, just outside the city walls, and building work soon began, masterminded by royal mason William Wallace. The result was a perfect expression of the northern Renaissance: a classically symmetrical Italianate palace, embellished with distinctively Scottish ornamentation. Construction was delayed by the Civil War, but the school finally took its first 30 pupils in 1659. Now a thriving co-educational public school, it still reserves 5 per cent of its places for 'foundationers'.

The original exterior, with its ogee-domed turrets and elegant chimneys, is much as it always was, except that the main entrance has been moved. The building was designed to be approached from the city, and to fully appreciate it visitors should walk round to the splendid north doorway with its delightful frieze of illustrative carvings. One scene shows the founder at work in his forge, another five pious young scholars in their uniforms. A life-size sculpture of Heriot presides over the fine arcaded courtyard; the inscription above it translates as 'This statue shows my body, this building my soul'. Today, he might add 'Please don't call it Hogwart's!'

Address Lauriston Place, EH3 9EQ, +44 (0)131 229 7263 | **Getting there** Lothian Buses 23, 27, 37, 45 or 47, or McGill's Bus 60 to Lauriston Place | **Hours** Normally viewable from outside only; email enquiries@george-heriots.com to enquire about visiting | **Tip** The Jinglin' Geordie is a characterful old pub with a jaunty sign featuring a painting of Heriot. It's about ten minutes' walk north-east of the school on Fleshmarket Close, a steep, narrow alley that leads from Cockburn Street to Market Street.

41 Gilmerton Cove

A subterranean rock-cut mystery

The former mining community of Gilmerton, on the south-eastern edge of Edinburgh, is the unlikely setting for one of the most fascinating, though little-visited places in the whole city. An old blacksmith's cottage on the main street has been turned into a visitor centre, with access to an extraordinary cluster of man-made caves and passages concealed three metres beneath it. The underground complex was originally lit by openings to the sky, but these have long since been covered over, and electric lighting now helps you find your way around.

You are immediately struck by the scale of the place, and the shape and texture of the womb-like walls, all hewn out of the living rock with tiny strokes of a chisel. But what's even more surprising is the built-in furniture, including long benches and tables, gently curving and beautifully cut from the solid sandstone. One of the tables is horn-shaped, and has a deep concave bowl cut into it. It's as if the Flintstones' house had been remodelled by a designer from 20th-century Milan.

Stories abound that the mysterious cove was once a hideaway for Covenanters, a gathering place for the Knights Templar or a den for a Hellfire Club. It has certainly been reused over the centuries, but its original, ancient purpose is unknown. Records show that a blacksmith, George Paterson, used it from 1724 to 1737, and his quite unfeasible claim to have spent just five years hewing out the complex himself was long accepted. In fact what he probably did was to clear out some of the soil and rubble deposited there at a much earlier date. New research, using ground-penetrating radar, has now revealed further, extensive subterranean passages and chambers, yet to be explored, beyond a blocked tunnel. Gilmerton Cove might one day be proved to be a sacred prehistoric site – perhaps a Druid temple – created long before the settlement of Edinburgh.

Address 16 Drum Street, EH17 8QH | Getting there Lothian Buses 3, 29, X29 or 400 to Gilmerton; the Cove is accessed from the Visitor Centre, in a cottage next door to Ladbroke's | Hours The Cove is temporarily closed to the public while a group from the local community work to resolve issues caused by water penetration. It is aimed to reopen it soon, under new management. | Tip To see later manifestations of underground Edinburgh, visit the 18th-century South Bridge vaults, accessed from Blair Street in the Old Town; see www.mercattours.com for information.

42 Gladstone's Land

From pigsties to painted ceilings

In the Old Town's 17th-century heyday, the High Street and Lawnmarket were at the core of a prosperous boomtown. Constrained by its medieval walls, the teeming city was forced to expand upwards, and visitors marvelled at the immense height of the buildings, some of which reached 14 storeys. They were also amazed at the great number of individuals of all social classes who lived quite literally on top of each other, from the wealthiest on the first floor to the poorest in the garret.

Easily missed among the tawdry tourist traps that now punctuate the Royal Mile is one well-preserved tenement, which has been sympathetically restored to give an authentic insight into life there 400 years ago. The six-storey Gladstone's Land is named after the merchant Thomas Gledstanes, who bought it in 1617. (The gilded hawk on the sign outside alludes to his name: 'gled' is the old Scots word for the red kite.) Its narrow frontage has two features once common along the old High Street – an external staircase for access to upper floors, and a ground-floor arcade leading to a 'luckenbooth', or shop, behind (now a café and ice-cream parlour). The arcades sheltered traders and passers-by as well as livestock – pigs, which fed on waste littering the streets, were often kept in pens under the stair.

Many original fixtures survive in the tenement's interior, including fireplaces, flooring, and wood beamed ceilings with delightful decorative painting. The first-floor rooms are furnished in period style, most impressively with a fine four-poster bed, and the well-informed guides give vivid accounts of how the diverse tenants who stayed in the building would have used each room. It's all remarkably atmospheric, and looking out through the tiny half-shuttered windows, you almost expect to see Gledstanes' cook haggling with a fishwife, or the minister from the next apartment picking his way gingerly through the clamour of the pungent streets.

Address 477B Lawnmarket, EH1 2NT, +44 (0)131 226 5856, www.nts.org.uk | Getting there Lothian Buses 9, 23 or 27 to George IV Bridge | Hours Daily, self-guided visits 10am–3pm (last entry 2.30pm), guided tours 3pm | Tip Gladstone's Land is owned by the National Trust for Scotland, who let out the upper floors as four comfortable and well-equipped holiday flats; see NTS website for information.

43 Glencorse Reservoir

Still waters and deep history

The low, green Pentland Hills are known as Edinburgh's lungs. Just a few miles south-west of the city, they're remarkably easy to escape to for a breath of fresh air. They're also a major source of that other essential element – water – and the reservoir of Glencorse, the earliest of several that serve the city, can be reached in a short walk that is both refreshing and intriguing.

You start at Flotterstone Inn, from where a wide track leads up past peaceful woods and fields. The landscape appears timeless, but it has in fact been shaped for centuries by the influence of man. The hill of Castle Law to the north is modified by 2,000-year-old earthworks, the remains of an extensive fort occupied by the Votadini tribe. Even more surprisingly, the lovely tree-fringed expanse of water that you soon reach was created less than two centuries ago.

Since 1676, Edinburgh's water supply had been piped in from springs three miles away at Comiston, but by the early 19th century the growing city was in dire need of another clean and abundant source. The brilliant civil engineer James Jardine had already directed two major projects to enhance the urban environment – the drainage of the Nor' Loch and the Burgh Loch to create Princes Street Gardens and the Meadows – when in 1819 he was tasked with building a reservoir to retain the waters of Glencorse Burn. He constructed a vast earth dam, with filter beds that can still be seen among the pinewoods, and a pipeline over nine miles long to carry the water to a huge tank on Edinburgh's Castlehill.

Submerged beneath Glencorse's waters are the remains of the 13th-century chapel of St Catherine, built by Sir William St Clair, legendarily after he won the land in a wager with King Robert the Bruce over whose hunting dogs would bring down a prized white deer. It's said that in rare hot spells when the water is low, the bell from its tower can be heard tolling faintly from the depths.

Address Flotterstone, Penicuik, EH26 0PP | **Getting there** Houston's Coaches 101/102 from St Andrew Square Bus Station to Flotterstone Inn on the A 702 (about 40 minutes). Walk 100 yards up the road behind the inn to the Pentlands Regional Park Information Centre, which has maps of the routes available, or simply follow the signposted track to Glencorse. | **Tip** The reservoir has a trout fishery; no bank fishing is allowed but boats may be booked in advance; see www.glencorsersv.co.uk for details.

44 Glenkinchie Distillery

Tak aff yer dram

Edinburgh was long famed for the distinctive odour of its breweries; what's less well known is that a great deal of whisky also used to be made in the city. As well as hundreds of illegal stills, there were at least 12 licensed whisky distilleries operating here in the late 19th century. The last of these, Glen Sciennes in Newington, closed in 1925, but you don't have to travel too far out of town today to find the place which, since 1989, has adopted the mantle of maker of the Edinburgh Malt.

Glenkinchie Distillery is about 15 miles east of the city, in rolling farmland near the village of Pencaitland. Founded in 1837, it was rebuilt in the 1890s, and now produces nearly three million litres of whisky per year. Its visitor centre has an informative and well-mounted exhibition that includes a splendid, vast scale model of a distillery, made in 1925 and formerly on display at London's Science Museum. But a tour of the actual premises is essential if you want to get a real feel for the process of whisky production. Several options are available, including evening events.

The distillery is a much leaner operation than it once was. Many of the processes have been automated, and it no longer malts its own grain, though most of the barley used is still grown locally in the surrounding countryside of East Lothian, north of the lovely Lammermuir Hills, the source of the crystal clear streams that still supply all the water used. But despite the machinery and banks of computers, the building reeks of atmosphere and tradition. This is largely due to the continuous, rich aroma of the fermentation taking place in the huge wooden washback tubs, two made of Oregon pine, four of Canadian larch, and the pair of magnificent, fat-bellied copper stills, the largest of their type in Scotland. The end product is a fresh, light, fragrant Lowland malt, which you must of course sample in a tutored tasting at the end of your tour.

Address by Pencaitland, Tranent, EH34 5ET, +44 (0)1875 342 012, www.malts.com/distilleries/glenkinchie | **Getting there** By car, 45 minutes' drive from Edinburgh via A 68 and A 6093; Eve Coaches 123 from Haddington to Glenkinchie | **Hours** Daily, May–Sept 10am–6pm, Oct–Apr 10am–5pm; see website for tour times and booking | **Tip** For an unusual range of whiskies, with tastings offered by knowledgeable staff, try Cadenhead's Whisky Shop, run by Scotland's oldest independent bottler (172 Canongate, EH8 8DF, Mon–Sat 10.30am–5.30pm).

45 Greyfriars Kirkyard

Much more than a legendary dog's home

The sentimental tale of Bobby, the faithful Skye terrier who refused to leave his master's grave for an unfeasible 14 years, attracts thousands of visitors to Greyfriars. Many are content to pay homage to his bronze statue, which sits on a granite pillar opposite the main entrance to the churchyard. But those who make their way up the short close at the top of Candlemaker Row and through the gates have a great deal more of interest in store than the dubious relics of a Victorian shaggy dog story.

Greyfriars Kirkyard is one of the most atmospheric places in Edinburgh, a tree-studded, sloping grassy acre with a timeless air of mystery. The funereal gloom has been largely pushed to the sides – the result of a town council decree in the early 17th century, which allowed the development of the existing graveyard on condition that memorials were only erected against the walls. This had the effect of giving stone carvers the freedom to work on a much grander scale than usual, and resulted in some of the most vivid and original sculpture in Scotland at that time. The weathering of the centuries seems only to enhance the impact of its lively and often arrestingly eerie imagery.

Many illustrious and notorious figures are buried beneath these ornate monuments, from pioneering architect William Adam to hanging judge George Mackenzie. It was also in Greyfriars, in 1638, that thousands of Presbyterians defied the authority of King Charles I by signing the National Covenant, in protest against new English forms of worship. During the persecution that followed, hundreds of them were imprisoned in an open enclosure within the cemetery, where many perished.

A few of the graves are protected by substantial iron grids, secured with padlocks. Known as mortsafes, these were designed to prevent the disturbance of newly interred corpses by grave robbers (to say nothing of four-pawed intruders).

Address 26a Candlemaker Row, EH1 2QQ, www.greyfriarskirk.com | Getting there Lothian Buses 2, 9, 23, 27, 35 or 45 to Forrest Road | Hours Unrestricted | Tip The kirkyard has recently become hugely popular with Harry Potter fans, though direct connections with the books are elusive, to say the least. Maps of the gravestones are available in the shop by the main gate. Greyfriars Kirk itself has a fine acoustic and is a regular concert venue. It also has a small museum.

46 The GVIR Postbox at the Inch

Defusing an explosive situation

The UK Post Office introduced their sturdy wayside pillar boxes in the 1850s, when Queen Victoria was on the throne, and these cast iron repositories of the Royal Mail have since then carried the insignia of the monarch reigning at the time of their installation. But Edinburgh's Inch Estate has one that is different. The pillar box standing modestly near the corner of Walter Scott Avenue and Gilmerton Road was erected in February 1953, yet it bears the Latin cypher of GVIR, for King George VI – who had by then been dead for a year. The story of how this anomaly came about is unexpectedly explosive.

When the young Queen Elizabeth acceded to the throne in 1952, the new Inch housing scheme was nearing completion, and it was decided that the first post box in Scotland to be embossed with the symbol of EIIR, for Elizabeth the Second, would be installed there in an official ceremony on 28 November. But this symbol was a contentious issue. Many Scots questioned the legality of the new queen's title, which they felt showed an arrogant disregard for their nation's independent history: the English Queen Elizabeth I had reigned before the Union of the Crowns, and was never the ruler of Scotland.

There was police presence at the unveiling of the post box, but 36 hours later the royal symbol was defaced with tar. More serious protests followed, including the planting of makeshift bombs, and an attack on the numerals with a sledgehammer. The damage was repaired, but finally, on 12 February, 1953, the postbox was completely blown apart by gelignite. Though responsibility was claimed by two republican organisations, no one was ever prosecuted, and it was quickly replaced with an old one marked GVIR, which still stands. Since this incident, all new post boxes north of the border have simply displayed the Scottish Crown.

Address Opposite 249 Gilmerton Road, EH16 5TT | Getting there Lothian Buses 3, 8 or 29 to Gilmerton Road (Walter Scott Avenue) | Tip An unexpected sight in the grounds of the University Landscaping Department at 20 Gilmerton Road is a large, well-preserved medieval pigeon-house. Originally on the estate of the 17th-century Inch House, Nether Liberton Doocot has 2,072 nesting holes.

47 I J Mellis Cheesemongers

Savour the subtle flavours

Few Edinburgh people had heard the term 'cheesemonger' before Iain Mellis came to town. It was 1993, and supermarkets had long since reduced the general experience of cheese to little more than rubbery orange Cheddar, and desiccated Parmesan sawdust. Mellis set out to change all that. He'd worked as a cheesemaker for 15 years, and had become increasingly frustrated by the lack of retail outlets for the farmhouse cheeses produced in the UK. Inspired by the specialist *fromageries* of France, and by photographs of old-fashioned grocery stores, he set up shop with his wife Karen in a small, tunnel-like vault in Victoria Street. Local restaurants were immediate customers, as well as the cheese-starved public, and soon there were two more branches in Edinburgh, and three in other Scottish cities. In 2018, the Mellises' eldest son Rory joined the team, and expanded the business's online market.

It's not just the look of the premises that's traditional, but the principles of quality and service. The well-informed staff are all artisan cheese enthusiasts, who are delighted to advise on everything from correct storage to ordering a cheese wedding cake. First-time visitors are often amazed at the number of British and Irish artisan cheeses on display – not just Stiltons and Cheddars, but cow, sheep and goat varieties of every style, all carefully brought to maturity in the temperature-controlled warehouse before they go on sale. The stock of Scottish cheeses has grown in recent years as the number of small specialist producers has increased, and includes varieties for all tastes, ranging from nutty Connage Gouda to tangy Hebridean Blue, by way of crumbly Anster and creamy Blackmount. There are also classic continental favourites imported directly from producers, and a select range of other quality deli fare. The shop has had several makeovers over the years, but it has never lost its own particular atmosphere and charm, or the values that made it so special three decades ago.

Address 30a Victoria Street, EH1 2JW, +44 (0)131 226 6215, www.mellischeese.net (also at 6 Baker's Place, EH3 6SY & 330 Morningside Road, EH10 4QJ) | Getting there Lothian Buses 9, 23 or 27 to George IV Bridge (Victoria Street) | Hours Daily, but variable; check website for current details | Tip Just across the road from the Victoria Street shop, the Bow Bar is a traditional, no-music pub with well-kept real ales, a terrific array of whiskies, and excellent bartenders (80 West Bow, www.thebowbar.co.uk).

48 Inchcolm

Ancient battleground in the Forth

With two sandy beaches and a well-preserved medieval abbey, the tiny hook-shaped Inchcolm (Columba's Isle) is the loveliest of the islands in the Firth of Forth. Its tranquillity is almost palpable – unless you stray into the seabirds' territory during the nesting season, when you'll find yourself the object of their aerial aggression. It seems the perfect place to escape from the turmoil of mainstream, mainland life. But Inchcolm hasn't always been so peaceful.

In 1123 a violent storm forced a ship carrying King Alexander I to its shores. The island had been a hermitage from early times, and the holy man then in residence took care of the royal party for several days. In gratitude, the king vowed to build a monastery on Inchcolm, and Augustinian brethren duly settled there shortly afterwards. Their priory flourished, and was raised to the status of an abbey in 1235.

Considering the havoc that they later endured, the monastic buildings, including the cloister, chapter house, refectory, and bell tower, have survived remarkably intact. Throughout the 14th century and beyond, the canons' lives of contemplation and prayer were repeatedly violated by English raiders, plundering and wreaking destruction. A Latin proverb inscribed on the wall of the warming room gives an insight into the stoical attitude of the community: it translates as 'It is foolish to fear what cannot be avoided'. The final indignity came with the Protestant Reformation in the 16th century, when the beleaguered monastery was phased out and its church dismantled.

But the island's turbulent history didn't end there. Its strategic position meant that it was in military use during the Napoleonic Wars, and again in both the world wars of the 20th century. The drabness of the remains from these conflicts contrasts sharply with the singular charm of the abbey, now an occasional venue for weddings.

Address Access via ferry from Hawes Pier, South Queensferry, EH30 9TB | Getting there Lothian Buses 43 to South Queensferry, or train from Edinburgh to Dalmeny and 10-minute walk. Two companies operate a ferry service to the island; for details see www.maidoftheforth.co.uk or www.forthtours.com | Hours Abbey: Apr–Sept, daily 10.30am–5pm, Oct, daily 10.30am–4pm (last entry 45 minutes beforehand) | Tip Buy a picnic to take with you before you leave Edinburgh – there's no café on the island. Pep & Fodder at 11 Waterloo Place is near Waverley Station, and has a good range of tasty options (daily 7.30am–4pm).

49 The Innocent Railway

When trains went at a horse's pace

It's an intriguing fact that the earliest railway in the capital was powered not by state-of-the-art locomotives, but the more user-friendly alternative of horses. In the 1820s the Edinburgh and Dalkeith Railway Company first proposed using steam trains to carry coal from the mines of Midlothian into the city centre, and out to the coast at Fisherrow. But the city was cautious about adopting this noisy and dangerous new means of transport.

Undaunted, the company revised their plans, incorporating wagons drawn by horses, and in 1831 they opened the first phase of their line. It included the UK's very first railway tunnel, bored through the hard igneous bedrock of Holyrood Park, just east of the terminus at St Leonard's.

The venture was a commercial success, and local businessman Michael Fox soon had the idea of introducing a passenger service, initially using old stagecoaches converted to run on the iron rails. It was immediately popular, carrying over 150,000 people in its first year of operation, and his enterprise was soon bought out by the company. It's hard to overstate the impact that this line had on the lives of the ordinary Edinburgh populace, able for the first time to take day trips out to the country or the seaside for a modest fare. There were no stations – passengers got on and off wherever they liked. Local chronicler Robert Chambers coined the name 'Innocent Railway' to evoke the simple pleasure of these leisurely journeys, where he never felt 'in the least jeopardy'.

This innocence was inevitably short lived, and in 1845 the line was taken over and converted to steam. The route finally closed in 1968, but part of it was later resurfaced as a path, and in 1994 a long stretch, including the 517-metre-long tunnel, became part of National Cycle Route 1. Its many two-wheeled users now easily reach speeds unthinkable in those far-off innocent days.

Address Join the cycle path at East Parkside, EH16 5XJ, the site of the former St Leonard's terminus; the Innocent Railway Tunnel is close by, just inside Holyrood Park | Getting there Lothian Buses 2, 30 or 33 to East Preston Street, then walk down Holyrood Park Road to East Parkside | Tip Take a walk in the park above the railway tunnel, along Duddingston Low Road, for a good view of the impressive outcrop of gigantic columnar basalt known as Samson's Ribs.

50_The International Climbing Arena

Taking rock sports to new heights

At first sight, Edinburgh's vast indoor climbing arena, the largest such facility in Europe, is both overwhelmingly daunting and irresistibly enticing. With its towering 30-metre walls, it's clearly no piece of cake – though to the uninitiated its candy-coloured spangles and pastel slices make it look curiously like one.

The arena was the brainchild of Edinburgh climbers Duncan McCallum and Rab Anderson, who in 1995 formed a company with architect David Taylor to convert a disused quarry into what was originally the Ratho Adventure Centre. Artificial climbing walls intended as training facilities for outdoor rock climbing had been built in the 1970s in a few Edinburgh colleges, but by the end of the 20th century the sport of indoor climbing was fast growing as a leisure pursuit in its own right. The Ratho team employed Austrian mountaineering experts to help design and build 2,500 square metres of plywood and resin climbing walls inside the quarry, and in 2003 the impressive five-storey building, complete with gym, health club, restaurant and conference centre, finally opened to the public. But problems with the construction soon came to light, and the following year it went into receivership. Rescued by the city council, it underwent a massive overhaul before reopening in 2007 as the Edinburgh International Climbing Arena.

Though originally designed mainly for the climbing elite, the arena now offers activities at all levels. The walls, fitted with over 11,000 bolt-on holds, have more than 300 colour-coded routes of varying difficulty, and bouldering – climbing on much smaller 'rocks', without ropes or harnesses – is a popular alternative. For daredevils there's the Aerial Assault Course, 30 metres above the ground, while others will prefer the gentler thrills of Clip 'n' Climb, open to all aged between 4 and 84.

Address EICA, South Platt Hill, Newbridge, EH28 8AA, +44 (0)131 333 6333, www.edinburghleisure.co.uk/venues/edinburgh-international-climbing-arena | **Getting there** Tram to Gyle Centre, then Lothian Buses 70 to Ratho (Canal Centre) and 15-minute walk west along towpath | **Hours** Climbing: Mon, Wed & Fri 10am–9pm, Tue & Thu 10am–10pm, Sat & Sun 9am–6pm | **Tip** Scotland's first inland surf resort, Lost Shore, opened in November 2024 on an extensive site next to the Climbing Arena. As well as Europe's largest wave pool, it features waterfront pods and lodges, a café and restaurant, and a wellness centre (www.lostshore.com).

51 The James Clerk Maxwell Birthplace

The forgotten giant of physics

Edinburgh could well have spawned many unsung geniuses, but the supreme contender for the title must surely be the 19th-century mathematical physicist James Clerk Maxwell. A major influence on Albert Einstein, Maxwell has a reputation within the scientific community that is unassailable, and has, if anything, grown in recent decades. This has led to many posthumous honours: his name graces several academic buildings, as well as the world's largest astronomical telescope, a mountain range on Venus, and the gap in Saturn's rings. But to the general public he remains a nonentity. This lack of recognition is especially undeserved in view of the massive effect his pioneering work has had in shaping our modern age. It was Maxwell's ground-breaking discovery of the laws of electrodynamics that paved the way for much of the everyday technology we all take for granted, from radio and television to mobile phones and microwave ovens. He even produced the world's first colour photograph – in 1861.

In 1993, the James Clerk Maxwell Foundation acquired the New Town house where this brilliant figure was born in 1831. They have now restored it to near its original state and set up a small museum with displays from their collections, including portraits and documents as well as fascinating material relating to Maxwell's early life. His keenly enquiring mind was evident by the age of three, when he began to show a precocious interest in the forces of nature, particularly those that govern light and movement. Later, at Edinburgh Academy, he was nicknamed 'Dafty' by his uncomprehending fellow pupils. There are charmingly vivid watercolours by his talented cousin Jemima Wedderburn, capturing some key moments in young James' boyhood in Scotland, and the original manuscript of a paper on geometry presented to Edinburgh's Royal Society, which he wrote at the age of just 14.

Address James Clerk Maxwell Foundation, 14 India Street, EH3 6EZ, www.clerkmaxwellfoundation.org | Getting there Lothian Buses 24 or 29 to Howe Street | Hours Normally Tue 3pm, plus some weekend afternoons. Advance booking essential, by email – see website for details | Tip The world's only public monument to Maxwell is the statue erected in 2008 at the east end of George Street in the city centre, the work of Sandy Stoddart (see ch. 52). The pedestal features classically themed reliefs representing Newton and Einstein conducting experiments with light.

52 The *Kidnapped* Statue

Lost and lonesome memorial to a literary giant

A shallow recess in a high wall by a thundering highway in the western suburbs seems an odd site for one of Edinburgh's finest public sculptures – all the more surprising since the monument in question was intended as a long-overdue grand memorial to one of the city's greatest sons, the internationally famed writer Robert Louis Stevenson. Its obscurity is compounded by the fact that this purpose is far from obvious, least of all to intrigued tourists who glimpse it from the airport bus, which stops a couple of metres away *en route* to the city centre. For the author himself appears only in a modest profile medallion on the plinth, beneath two colossal bronze figures in heroic pose and carefully rendered 18th-century clothing, and you have to locate the plaque on a nearby stone pier to discover that they represent David Balfour and Alan Breck Stewart, the principal characters in his 1886 novel *Kidnapped.*

Set soon after the Jacobite rising, this enduringly popular tale charts the thrilling adventures of the teenage Balfour and his friendship with Alan Breck, a charismatic rebel Highlander (and a real historical figure). The sculpture, by maverick neoclassicist Sandy Stoddart, stands near the spot on Corstorphine Hill where the two part company for the last time, leaving young Davie feeling 'so lost and lonesome' that he almost breaks down in tears. Breck holds aloft a wooden cross which plays an important part in the story.

Stoddart, a passionate advocate of 'serious monuments that don't have the *Braveheart* touch' suggested the subject when he was approached by Scottish & Newcastle Breweries to create a statue to mark their move in 1999 to new headquarters on Corstorphine Road, at the aptly named Balfour Stewart House. Siting it in a former entranceway on the edge of the grounds was meant to make the work accessible to a wide public, but though thousands hurtle past every day, few stop to look at it.

Address 46 Corstorphine Road, EH12 5PY (near junction with Ellersly Road) | Getting there Lothian Buses 12, 26, 31 or 100 to Western Corner | Hours Always accessible | Tip There are three other memorials to Stevenson in Edinburgh which also require some effort to find: a superb bronze bas-relief in St Giles' Cathedral by Irish-American sculptor Augustus Saint-Gaudens, based on a portrait modelled from life in 1887; a minimalist headstone by Ian Hamilton Finlay with the punning inscription *A Man of Letters/RLS*, erected in 1987 in Princes Street Gardens (near the Ross Fountain); and a statue by Alan Herriot depicting the author as a boy, unveiled in 2013 outside Colinton Parish Church.

53 The King's Gallery

Congenial venue for top-tier exhibitions

The artworks amassed over the centuries by the British monarchy constitute one of the largest and finest private collections in the world. There are more than a million items, many of them truly breathtaking: masterly paintings by Rembrandt and Vermeer, haunting drawings by Leonardo and Holbein, exquisite Mughal miniatures, rare Chinese ceramics, intricate Fabergé eggs – the list goes on and on. But very few of these treasures were ever put on public display until the reign of Elizabeth II, who in 1962 had a pavilion at Buckingham Palace converted into a gallery for temporary exhibitions. Four decades later, Scots were granted a share in this bounty when an equivalent venue was created at the Palace of Holyroodhouse, in celebration of her 2002 Golden Jubilee.

Renamed the King's Gallery after the accession of Charles III, the Edinburgh building occupies the shell of a 19th-century church and adjoining school, sympathetically remodelled by local architect Ben Tindall to form an attractive exhibition space with state-of-the-art lighting and climate control. Both the massively resplendent entrance gateway and the welcoming reception area incorporate specially commissioned works of art which announce the gallery's regal significance together with its aesthetic function, while the superbly crafted woodwork of the staircase and balcony creates an inviting and surprisingly intimate atmosphere.

It's not a vast space – it was never intended for unwieldly blockbuster shows – but it's ideal for the changing exhibitions of the Royal Collection, where the emphasis is on quality rather than quantity. Covering a huge range of themes, these are always immaculately curated and beautifully presented, and audio guides with illuminating commentary are included in the ticket price. There's also the option of converting your ticket into a pass which allows multiple return visits, free of charge, for the following year.

Address Palace of Holyroodhouse, Canongate, EH8 8DX, +44 (0)303 123 7306, www.rct.uk/visit/the-kings-gallery-palace-of-holyroodhouse | Getting there Lothian Buses 35 to Holyrood | Hours Daily, Apr–Sept 9.30am–6pm, Nov–Mar 9.30am–4.30pm (may vary – check website); last entry one hour beforehand | Tip The monarch's official residence in Scotland, the Palace of Holyroodhouse, is adjacent; even if you don't pay to tour its state apartments you can still visit the café in the historic mews courtyard, perfect for coffee, lunch or afternoon tea.

54 Lady Stair's House

The men behind the pen

Set back from the cramped frontages of the Lawnmarket is an unexpectedly spacious courtyard, which takes its name from one of the finest mansions of the Old Town. Built in 1622 by wealthy merchant Sir William Gray, the house was enlarged in the early 18th century when it became home to his granddaughter, Elizabeth, Dowager Countess of Stair, a vivacious and fashionable society lady, famed as the first person in the city to have a black manservant. Lady Stair's House was freely restored in 1897 in Arts and Crafts style, with picturesque turrets and a minstrels' gallery. It now houses the small but engrossing Writers' Museum, dedicated chiefly to the giants of Scottish literature: Robert Burns, Sir Walter Scott, and Robert Louis Stevenson.

Entered from a narrow turnpike stair, the open-plan main hall is flanked by a warren of rooms filled with a wealth of exhibits. Three very different personalities are vividly brought to life in displays of portraits, personal documents, and memorabilia, including the writing desks of both Scott and Burns. Scott's dining room has been recreated, and earlier possessions include a delightful chess set, and his rocking horse, with one footrest set higher than the other to counteract the effects of polio contracted in infancy. The section devoted to Burns contains letters and original manuscripts, as well as some haunting images of the handsome 'ploughman poet', and material relating to his more prosaic professions of land surveyor and exciseman.

Downstairs is the evocative Stevenson collection. There is a wardrobe from his childhood home made by the infamous Deacon Brodie – the inspiration for Jekyll and Hyde – and many intriguing items from his last years in Samoa, such as the talismanic silver and tortoiseshell ring he was wearing when he died. A gift from a local chief, it's inscribed 'Tusitala', meaning 'teller of tales'.

Address The Writers' Museum, 3 Lady Stair's Close, 477 Lawnmarket, EH1 2PA, +44 (0)131 529 4901, www.edinburghmuseums.org.uk/venue/writers-museum | **Getting there** Lothian Buses 9, 23 or 27 to George IV Bridge, then walk up Lawnmarket to Makars' Court – part of Lady Stair's Close – which has flagstones inscribed with quotations from Scottish writers | **Hours** Daily 10am–5pm | **Tip** Down the close at 322 Lawnmarket, Riddle's Court is a well-preserved 16th-century merchant's house, recently restored and now the Patrick Geddes Centre for Learning. It hosts a varied programme of educational events organised by the Scottish Historic Buildings Trust. Tours are available if booked in advance, and the venue can also be hired for weddings, conferences etc (www.shbt.org.uk/the-patrick-geddes-centre).

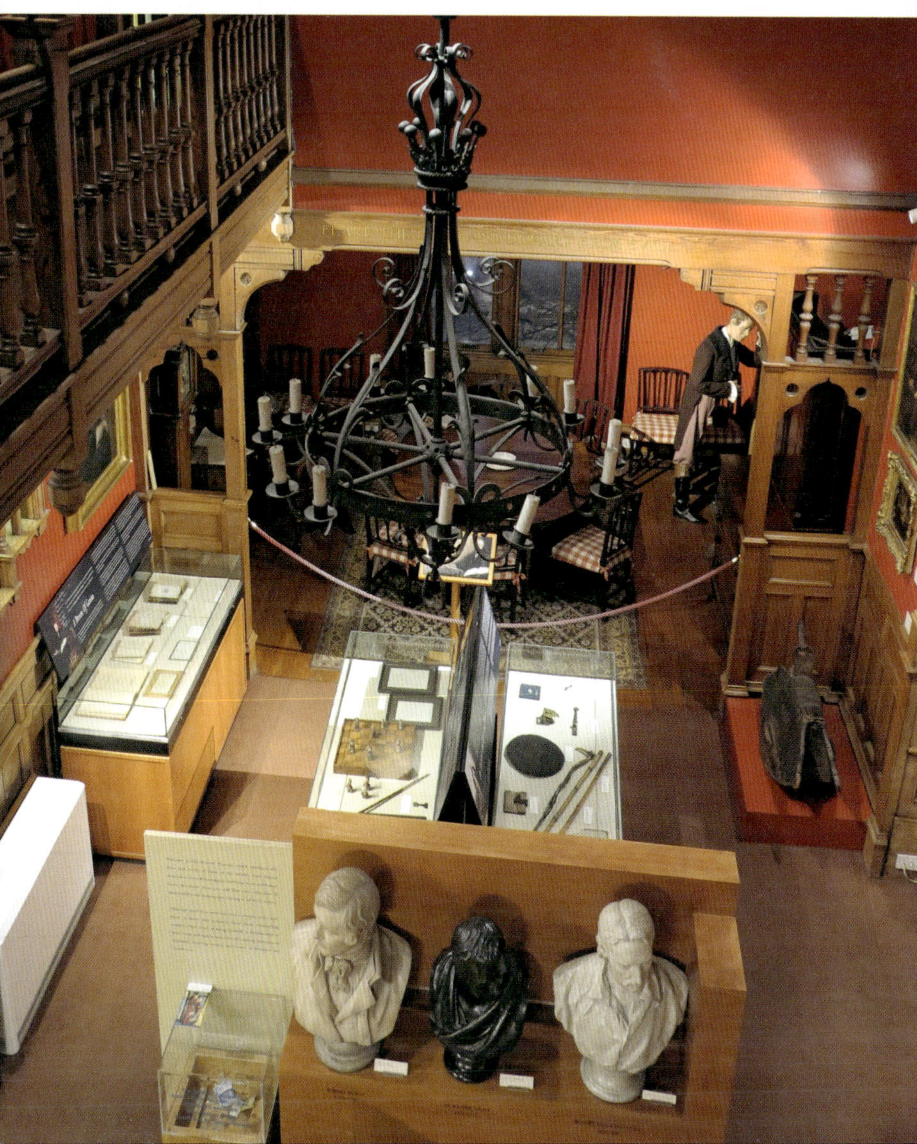

55 Lady Victoria Colliery

A mine of information

The capital's nickname of 'Auld Reekie' (Old Smokey) harks back to the days when the fuel that fired the industry of Scotland's central belt was also the only source of heating in city people's homes. The rich coal seams to the south and east of Edinburgh have been exploited for a very long time – the monks of Holyrood were given rights to an outcrop of 'black stanis' in the 12th century – and the showplace super-pit that was once the second largest colliery in Scotland is only nine miles from the city. Opened in 1895, the Lady Victoria Colliery has long since ceased production, but much of its four-acre complex has been preserved, and the site now houses the National Mining Museum.

The 'Lady Vic' – named after the wife of its developer, the Marquess of Lothian – was notable from its early days for its use of innovative technology, such as steel pit props and electrically powered equipment. During its 86 years of operation it produced a record 40 million tons of coal, all hauled up the 500-metre mineshaft by a massive steam-driven winding engine built in 1894. The community of Newtongrange became the largest mining village in the country, and a high, covered gantry, which still stands, was constructed across the busy A7 road to give the thousands of miners safe access to the pit.

The colliery was re-established as a museum shortly after its closure in 1981. Informative displays now explain everything from the prehistoric origins of coal to modern extraction methods, but for most visitors the highlight is their tour guide – all are ex-miners, with human stories to tell about the lives of workers at the coal face. The railway line built to service the colliery has recently been reopened, and the path from the station leads round the perimeter, allowing glimpses of the huge area closed to the public, with its silent, abandoned relics of the era when coal was king.

Address Newtongrange, EH22 4QN, +44 (0)131 663 7519, www.nationalminingmuseum.com | Getting there Train (Borders Railway), Edinburgh Waverley to Newtongrange (12 minutes); the museum is a few minutes' walk from the station | Hours Daily, Apr–Oct 10am–5pm, Nov–Mar 10am–4pm | Tip Take a longer trip on the Borders Railway to its terminus at Tweedbank, and visit the historic house and gardens of Abbotsford, home of Sir Walter Scott, a 20-minute walk or short bus ride from the station (www.scottsabbotsford.com).

56 Lauriston Castle

Edwardian time capsule with a long history

It's almost a century since Lauriston Castle last had a permanent resident – unless you count the mysterious ghostly lady whose shadowy presence is announced by the sound of her swishing silk dress. This grand country house has been kept as it was in 1926, but the history of the building goes back much further, and involves a couple of characters who would certainly make equally intriguing phantoms, should their spirits feel inclined to return.

The building that forms the core of the present house was commissioned around 1593 by the father of John Napier, the brilliant mathematician and physicist whose legacy includes the concept of logarithms. Napier was also an astrologer – a carving now on the outer wall is said to represent a horoscope cast by him for his brother – and was rumoured to dabble in alchemy.

Ownership of the estate later passed to another colourful figure – John Law, a gambler, adventurer, and pioneering economist who founded the central bank of France in 1716, and went on to preside over the catastrophic meltdown of the financial scheme known as the Mississippi Bubble.

Extended in the 1820s in Scottish baronial style, the tower was transformed into 'a most comfortable house', and in the 1840s the estate was artfully landscaped by the architect Playfair. Lauriston's last owner was William Reid, the wealthy proprietor of a local furniture firm. He bought it in 1902, and with his wife Margaret set about redesigning the interior and filling it with fashionable *objets d'art*, from Georgian Blue John ware and Italian *pietra dura* to the pastiche artworks known as Crossley wool mosaics. Their home was also furnished with the latest in bathroom fittings, courtesy of Margaret's brother, who ran a plumbing business. On her death, the estate was left to the nation on condition that nothing in the house was changed, and so it remains to this day.

Address 2a Cramond Road South, EH4 5QD, +44 (0)131 336 2060, www.edinburghmuseums.org.uk | Getting there Lothian Buses 47 to Davidson's Mains, then walk up Cramond Road South; alternatively 16, 27, 29, or 37 to Silverknowes Terminus and walk along Lauriston Farm Road | Hours House: guided tours only, Sat & Sun 1.30 & 3pm; advance booking essential – see website. Grounds: daily 8am–4.30pm; café & toilets: daily 10am–4pm | Tip Highlights of the Castle's extensive and peaceful park include a walk in the Japanese Friendship Garden, which celebrates the city's twinning with Kyoto, and watching the leisurely action on the lawns of the Edinburgh Croquet Club.

57_The Mansfield Traquair Centre

The rainbow at the end of the world

Just off the roundabout at the foot of Broughton Street stands a former church with an unremarkable Victorian exterior, which gives no clue to the magnificence within. Entering its vast nave is like stepping into a blaze of light. Apocalyptic biblical imagery illuminates the walls in a brilliant array of oranges, emeralds, sapphires and glistening gold. Multi-hued angels gather all around, sounding trumpets to accompany the heavenly choir, greeting risen souls and kneeling in adoration. It's Edinburgh's answer to the Sistine Ceiling, a herculean effort by a sole artist – in this case a woman.

There was a specific aim behind the realisation of this vision. The adherents of the Catholic Apostolic Church, founded in the 1830s, professed that the growing troubles of their time were all signs that the world was coming to an end. They believed that the contemplation of the second coming of Christ, which they thought to be imminent, would hold sins at bay, and prepare the soul for the Last Day. The Church evolved a new liturgy involving rich vestments, processions, music and incense. And in 1892 the Edinburgh congregation commissioned the 40-year-old, Irish-born artist Phoebe Anna Traquair to decorate their building with murals to enhance this ceremonial display.

She set about the task with intense energy, concentration and devotion, melding inspiration from painters such as Fra Angelico, Botticelli and William Blake, as well as ancient Celtic art, into her own personal style. Working only when the natural light was good enough, she took eight years to complete the cycle. Her unusual technique, based on oil paint mixed with beeswax, was quite sound, but in the late 20th century the building fell into disrepair, and the murals suffered. Now they have been expertly restored and can once more be enjoyed in all their glory, as if the world was after all nearing its end.

Address 15 Mansfield Place, EH3 6BB, www.mansfieldtraquair.org.uk | **Getting there** Lothian Buses 8 to Mansfield Place | **Hours** 2nd Sun of each month, 1–4pm; longer hours during the Edinburgh Festival | **Tip** For earthly sustenance, the Barony Bar, just up the road at 83–85 Broughton Street, is a characterful, unpretentious local, with real ale, traditional pub food, and an open fire.

58 The Meadows Sundial

Well-arranged time

The pleasant expanse of open grassland that borders the southern rim of the inner city was once the windswept, reedy Burgh Loch, one of the main sources of water for Edinburgh's Old Town. By the early 18th century it had become a marshy wasteland, and in 1722 local entrepreneur Thomas Hope undertook the task of draining it and creating a park with tree-lined avenues, where city residents soon flocked to take the air.

The Meadows, as it came to be known, enjoyed the most glorious moment in its history when for five months in 1886 it was the site of the International Exhibition of Industry, Science and Arts. This magnificent show included 20,000 exhibits, featuring everything from Clydeside locomotives to violins from Prague. There was a large-scale reconstruction of a medieval Edinburgh street, as well as an idealised dwelling house of the future. At its centre, filling half of the parkland, was a grand hall with a dome 36.5 metres high, and the whole event was illuminated by what was then a truly amazing array of 3,200 electric lamps.

Little evidence of the spectacle remains today. The famous archway of whale jawbones, from the Shetland and Fair Isle Knitters' Association, has now been removed. And few passers-by ever pause by the Meadows Sundial, although contemplation is invited by the mottoes carved on its sides: 'Man's days are as a shadow that passeth away', 'Well-arranged time is the surest sign of a well-arranged mind', and other appropriate homilies. Erected to commemorate the exhibition's opening by Queen Victoria's grandson, Prince Albert Victor, the sundial consists of a bronze armillary sphere on top of a tall octagonal column, built in courses of sandstone of different colours and types, each inscribed with the name of one of eight Edinburgh quarries. It's still flanked by two plane trees planted by the prince, though the elms that used to stand with them have long since died.

Address The Meadows, EH9 9EX; in the north-west corner, near the junction of Melville Drive and Lonsdale Terrace | Getting there Lothian Buses 24 to Leven Terrace | Tip Söderberg is an excellent Swedish bakery and café business, famed for its breads, buns, cakes and pizzas. It has no fewer than three branches within the Quartermile development, on the north side of the Meadows (www.soderberg.uk).

59_The Merchant Navy Memorial

Sustaining this island fortress

The fact that the British Merchant Navy suffered a death toll during both World Wars I and II that was greater than that of the Royal Navy is not generally realised. A combined total of over 42,000 merchant seamen died during these conflicts, while carrying out the highly dangerous task of transporting troops, armaments, food and merchandise between the UK and destinations around the globe. Their sacrifice, in war as well as in peacetime, is commemorated in this restrained, dignified monument, the work of local sculptor Jill Watson, which was unveiled in 2010.

As you approach the memorial, your attention is caught first by the large bronze sculpture, based on the Merchant Navy crest, at the top of the five-metre-high stone pillar – great bows of ships, one with a golden figurehead, some with billowing sails, embarking on their journeys to the four corners of the world. The closer you get, the more detail you can make out in the sensitive bronze plaques set into the column's sides, scenes on a tiny scale, as if diminished by the vast loneliness of the ocean. There's a distant view of New York City, and another of a lighthouse on a rocky island. A ship is dramatically blown apart, and a lifebelt, itself wrecked and torn, floats empty on the waves. Around a ledge lower down, the seamen are shown performing their daily tasks. One throws a rope, and the sailor about to catch it holds his hands together in what looks like an act of prayer. In a quietly understated way, Jill Watson has captured a huge range of human emotions.

Set in a beautifully laid circular pavement, the monument stands opposite the former Seamen's Home, on the waterfront of the inner harbour of Leith, Edinburgh's main trading port for 700 years. What was once a hub of maritime activity is now a peaceful spot to stand and look, remembering the selfless courage of so many individuals.

Address Tower Place, The Shore, EH6 7BZ | **Getting there** Lothian Buses 16, 34, 35 or 36 to The Shore | **Tip** The grand neoclassical Custom House at 67 Commercial Street has recently been restored, and is now a venue for exhibitions and events (+44 (0)131 220 1232).

60_The Millennium Clock

Towering circles of life and death

Every hour on the hour, the hubbub in the main hall of the National Museum of Scotland is stilled by the solemn opening notes of a Bach organ concerto – the signal that the Millennium Clock is coming to life. As it begins to erupt into five minutes of organised chaos, it's clear that this immense sculptural machine is rather more than a monumental timepiece. There's a clamour of tolling bells, clanking chains and frenetic movement as a multitude of wheels whirr into action, and shafts of coloured light illuminate a fantastic assembly of carved wooden figures – mischievous beasts, benign spirits and tormented human beings, all engaged in comical and tragic activity.

It was the idea of Julian Spalding, then director of Glasgow Museums, to commemorate the passing of 1,000 years of human history by commissioning the Scottish-based Russian kinetic sculptor Eduard Bersudsky to construct a vast animated clock tower. Like a master craftsman in a medieval cathedral, Bersudsky worked on the ambitious scheme in collaboration with an expert team – chief among them wood sculptor Tim Stead, glass artist Annica Sandström and clockmaker Jurgen Tübbecke. Thanks to funding from the National Lottery, the project was finally realised by the capital's National Museum in time for its inauguration there at noon on 1 January, 2000.

A unique gallimaufry of characters inhabit the tiers of the 10-metre-high tower. Some figures inevitably stand out – the cunning monkey who sets everything in motion; the reptilian-tailed Hitler and Stalin; the Chaplinesque tramp; the wheel of 12 desperate souls slowly proceeding on their cyclical journey; the lone woman at the summit, carrying the body of a man. Keen-eyed spectators can even spot themselves in the heart of the throng – the pendulum that swings erratically to and fro, with a grinning skeleton perched on top, is a giant convex mirror.

Address National Museum of Scotland, Chambers Street, EH1 1JF, +44 (0)300 123 6789, www.nms.ac.uk; the Clock is on display in the Collecting Stories Gallery, Level 1 | Getting there Lothian Buses 35 or 45 to Chambers Street, or 9, 23 or 27 to George IV Bridge | Hours Daily 10am–5pm; the Clock comes to life on the hour from 11am to 4pm throughout the day | Tip Don't miss the chance to see the world's first cloned mammal, Dolly the sheep (or at least a taxidermal version of her), on show in the Museum's Science and Technology Galleries.

61 The Miller Mausoleum

Craigentinny's marvellous marbles

There are many incongruous structures to be found in Edinburgh's streets – particularly at Festival time – but the most surreal juxtaposition of all can be seen year-round in a quiet 1930s' housing estate. Towering majestically above the pebbledashed bungalows of Craigentinny is a 15-metre-high mausoleum that would look more at home on the ancient Appian Way in Rome.

The story of the man for whom it was built, long before the bungalows appeared, is equally bizarre. William Henry Miller was a rich landowner and MP (for the English constituency of Newcastle-under-Lyme) who spent most of his time at his country house in Berkshire, indulging his passion for collecting antique books. He was a reclusive character, rarely seen in Edinburgh, yet on his death in 1848 his will revealed extraordinary instructions for his burial on his estate here, in what was then open fields. He left the vast sum of £20,000 to pay for the construction of a grand monument, covering a stone-lined shaft six metres deep leading down to his tomb, where a massive stone slab was to be placed on top of his coffin. Rumours soon began to circulate about the eccentric who seemed so anxious to conceal his own remains – he was said to have been a woman posing as a man, or even a hermaphrodite, though in all probability he simply had an exaggerated fear of body snatchers.

The mausoleum was not completed until 1856, and it was a further 11 years before the sculpted reliefs, by the Rome-based Alfred Gatley, were added. Despite their esoteric subject matter – 'The Song of Moses and Miriam' and 'The Overthrow of Pharoah in the Red Sea' – they were widely admired, and comparison with the famous Greek sculptures appropriated by Lord Elgin led to their being dubbed 'The Craigentinny Marbles'. Local residents today talk affectionately of their hidden treasure, which is proudly depicted on the neighbouring bowling club's insignia.

Address 3c Craigentinny Crescent, EH7 6QA | Getting there Lothian Buses 21 to Craigentinny Avenue, or 15, 26 or 45 to Portobello Road | Tip Miller's Edinburgh home, the 17th-century Craigentinny House, is about half a mile back into town at 9 Loaning Road. Now a community centre, with an unfortunate modern extension, it's still worth viewing from the outside.

62_The Moray Estate

A grand alternative to the monotonous grid

Edinburgh's New Town began to take shape in 1767, when the bold rectilinear plan of James Craig won the competition to design a residential suburb on the plain to the north of the old city. Despite some initial reluctance to occupy the site, by the end of the century the gridiron bordered by Princes Street and Queen Street had become *the* fashionable place to live, and in 1802 plans were drawn up for a second, larger phase of construction, which expanded the grid further north, to create a series of streets later derided by R. L. Stevenson as 'draughty parallelograms'.

To the west was a large pocket of open land bordered by the Water of Leith, the property of the 10th Earl of Moray. Though sloping and oddly shaped, the site was clearly ripe for 'the formation of a third grand division', and in 1822 the Earl commissioned designs for what he was determined should be the most splendid residential development in the city. Architect J. Gillespie Graham came up with an ingenious plan with three majestic curved streets – a crescent, an oval and a polygon – connected by short avenues and ornamented with private gardens. Strict planning rules governed the development of the estate: purchasers were charged five guineas for detailed drawings of the elevation of each home, and their builders had to adhere to a list of requirements ranging from the choice of stone to the pattern of the iron railings. Lord Moray showed his pride in the scheme by taking one of the most palatial houses, 28 Moray Place, for himself.

This grandest of New Town locales is still largely residential, highly desirable, and remarkably unaltered today. But its construction came at a price that was not merely monetary. Years later, the author Lord Cockburn wistfully remembered hearing the nocturnal calls of the corncrakes 'nestling in the dewy grass' of the lush green meadow that was sacrificed.

Address The chief streets of the estate are Randolph Crescent, Ainslie Place, Moray Place, and Doune Terrace. | **Getting there** Lothian Buses 19, 22, 36, 37, 43, 47 or 113 to Queensferry Street (Drumsheugh Place), then walk to Randolph Crescent to begin your tour | **Tip** Kay's Bar at 39 Jamaica Street, a few minutes' walk east in the more modest northern New Town, is a cosy little pub housed in a Victorian wine merchant's premises. It has a good range of real ales and malt whiskies, and serves bar food at lunchtime.

63_Moray House Garden Pavilion

The unspeakable act in the summerhouse

Just beyond the entrance to the car park of the University's School of Education is what looks like an oddly positioned gatehouse. No one would ever guess that this forlorn and permanently shuttered little gazebo was the purported site of one of the most significant events in Scottish history: the signing of the Act of Union with England.

Though political unification had been debated for over a century, the enactment of the Treaty of Union in 1707 did not go at all smoothly; the majority of the Scottish populace believed – with some justification – that pro-unionists had been 'bought and sold for English gold'. Daniel Defoe, later the author of *Robinson Crusoe*, was then employed as a secret agent by the English government. He reported that only one Scot in a hundred was in favour of the pact with England, and wrote vivid accounts of the unrest in the capital, where enraged mobs roamed the streets yelling 'No union!'

It was against this highly charged backdrop that the Lord Chancellor of Scotland, Viscount Seafield, proceeded to ratify the treaty. Seafield was then tenant of Moray House, a grand 17th-century mansion on the Canongate, renowned for its extensive terraced gardens. The story goes that the unionist faction had met to sign the Act in a High Street cellar when they became anxious about the mob outside, and decided to continue somewhere more discreet. In the lower terrace of the Chancellor's garden there was the ideal place – a secluded stone pavilion where the rabble couldn't reach them.

Moray House later became a teacher training college, and as it expanded, the garden disappeared. But the pavilion remained, and in 1911 it was totally renovated. However, despite – or perhaps because of – the recent revival of interest in the history of the union, it's generally ignored, and never open to the public.

Address Moray House School of Education, Holyrood Road, EH8 8AQ; the pavilion is just inside the gates of the vehicle entrance, to the east of the main building | Getting there Lothian Buses 35 to Canongate or McGill's Buses 60 to Holyrood Road (Viewcraig Street) | Hours Viewable from the outside only | Tip Another small historic building with an unexpected function can be found in Tweeddale Court, a wynd on the south side of the High Street, near the World's End pub. It's a storage shed for sedan chairs, the favourite mode of transport through the dirty, crowded streets of the Old Town for wealthy folk of the 17th and 18th centuries.

64_The Mound

The mud heap with an electric blanket

It may seem perverse that the inhabitants of a city so well endowed with hills as Edinburgh should spend five decades building an artificial one, but that's just what happened between 1781 and 1830. The Mound began as a makeshift causeway of stones and planks, bridging the swamp that later became Princes Street Gardens, and linking the Lawnmarket with the burgeoning New Town – the desirable housing development north of Princes Street. This was the brainchild of an Old Town tailor, George Boyd, who saw the advantage of providing customers there with direct access to his shop.

It was soon realised that 'Geordie Boyd's Mud Brig' was an ideal place to dispose of the massive quantities of soil and rubble being excavated for the construction of the New Town, and some two million cartloads were eventually emptied there. Residents of the insanitary Old Town also found the area a convenient refuse dump.

The growing 'Earthen Mound' soon attracted development. In 1800 the Bank of Scotland chose the top of the heap as the site for its headquarters, while hawkers' booths and sideshows occupied the lower slopes. Before the two temples of art that now grace the north end were completed, pictorial entertainment was to be found in a huge rotunda featuring dioramas of famous battles and exotic lands. In the 1830s, after much discussion, the Mound was landscaped according to the plan of Thomas Hamilton, and in 1846 the first railway tunnel was cut through it, to allow access to the new Waverley Station.

In 1959, a heating element was installed under the surface of the S-bend road, which was switched on in winter to prevent the asphalt from icing. A vast mesh comprising 37 miles of wire, it needed its own substation – still in West Princes Street Gardens. Though long since defunct, the Mound's 'electric blanket' lives on in Edinburgh lore.

Address The Mound, EH1 1YZ; it leads south about halfway along Princes Street | **Getting there** Lothian Buses 9, 23 and 27 all have routes that include the Mound | **Tip** Just inside the entrance to West Princes Street Gardens is the Floral Clock, a vast timepiece covered in and surrounded by tens of thousands of plants. Commissioned in 1903, it's the oldest of its kind in the world, and is replanted every spring. A cuckoo pops out from its house to call on the hour.

65 Mr Wood's Fossils

When Stan met Lizzie

The curious little shop at the southeastern corner of the Grassmarket has been trading for almost 40 years. But that's barely the twinkling of an eye compared with the age of its stock. Mr Wood's Fossils sells the solid evidence of living things from unimaginably ancient times; each piece is unique, many are exquisite, and prices start at less than you'd pay for a pint of beer in any of the nearby hostelries.

The remarkable self-taught palaeontologist Stan Wood started his business in Livingston in 1983, and opened his Edinburgh shop four years later. A former shipyard worker turned insurance salesman, Stan took up fossil hunting as a hobby in his early thirties, and discovered that he had an exceptional gift for it. His work gained him the respect of professional academics, and before long he was selling his finds to scientific institutions worldwide. In 1984 he made his most famous discovery in an old limestone quarry west of Edinburgh – a 340-million-year-old creature, 20 centimetres long, which he nicknamed Lizzie the Lizard. The specimen forced a total rethink of reptilian evolution, and was bought for £190,000 by the Royal Museum of Scotland. Stan's career continued with other astonishing finds, including the head of a giant scorpion, the largest invertebrate then known, and the 330-million-year-old Bearsden Shark, found while out walking his dog. Latterly, his discoveries in the Borders filled the huge hiatus in the fossil record known as Romer's Gap, and he was working on these when he died in 2012.

Stan's one-time assistant Matt Dale, a knowledgeable and enthusiastic geologist, has run the shop since 2008. Alongside a vast selection of fossils great and small from around the globe, he now stocks spectacular minerals and gemstones of every hue and – as if the ancient products of one planet weren't awe-inspiring enough – fragments of truly otherworldly meteorites.

Address 5 Cowgatehead, Grassmarket, EH1 1JY, +44 (0)131 220 1344, www.mrwoodsfossils.co.uk | Getting there Lothian Buses 2 to Grassmarket | Hours Mon–Thu 9am–4pm, Fri–Sun 10am–5.30pm | Tip Round the corner in the Cowgate, look out for the spire of the half-hidden Magdalen Chapel, originally part of a 16th-century almshouse. It contains the only pre-Reformation Scottish stained glass to survive in its original location (41 Cowgate, +44 (0)131 220 1450, currently open by appointment only).

66_Muschat's Cairn

The stones tell the tale

The huge area enclosed by Holyrood Park has a very long and varied history, and many old traditions live on in the names of its natural and man-made features. Hunter's Bog, Hagg's Knowe and the Wells o' Wearie are just a few of the evocative places still known to some natives, but one site that seldom attracts interest today is the low heap of boulders known as Muschat's Cairn. The story of this cairn is doubly sad, both for what it originally commemorated and for its subsequent ignominious treatment.

Cairns – mounds of stones deliberately placed as a memorial or landmark – are a common feature of remote Highland places, but it's much less usual to find one in a city context. This one was first built in 1720 by local people at the site of the vicious murder of young Ailie Muschat. Her husband Nicol, a failed surgeon, had taken her for a late evening walk in the park with the grim aim of getting rid of her; his profession must have supplied the necessary weapon, since it was reported that he almost severed her head in his violence. At his trial, his only defence was that he'd tired of her; he had previously involved a friend in an attempt to frame her with false accusations of adultery, and had then tried to poison her. Muschat was later hanged in the Grassmarket.

The murder site gained international fame when, in 1818, Walter Scott featured the cairn as the meeting place of the heroine Jeannie Deans and outlaw George Staunton in his popular historical novel *The Heart of Midlothian*. By then the stones had actually been removed, to make way for a footpath, but interest was such that in 1823 the town council decided to erect a new version, on a more convenient site a few hundred yards away. They made a decidedly botched job of it, using ugly boulders, and later repairing it with cement, but the municipal cairn is still there today – though few remember why.

Address Duke's Walk, Holyrood Park, EH8 7AT | **Getting there** Lothian Buses 4, 5, 15, 26, 44 or 45 to Meadowbank Stadium, then walk down Meadowbank Terrace; the cairn is just inside the park gateway | **Tip** Above the nearby St Margaret's Loch (an artificial pond created by Prince Albert) stand the gaunt ruins of St Anthony's Chapel. First recorded in 1426, when the pope gave money for its repair, it's built of three different local stones: black basalt, sandstone, and a volcanic green stone known as tuff.

67_The Museum of Scottish Fire Heritage

Blazing a trail for a life-saving service

Fire was a serious hazard in all medieval cities, but in the narrow closes and tall tenements of Edinburgh's Old Town it could be particularly devastating. Preventive measures were taken as early as 1426, when it was decreed that all citizens should have access to equipment such as 'cleikes' – long poles fixed with iron hooks for removing burning timbers. Four centuries later, Edinburgh was again at the forefront when in 1824 it established the first municipal fire service in the world, appointing 24-year-old James Braidwood as its Master. Only weeks into their training, his 80-strong team were severely tested in a massive five-day blaze that claimed the lives of two firemen. The lessons Braidwood learned helped him formulate an innovative methodology of firefighting that was soon adopted worldwide, and he went on to head London's first professional brigade.

With such a legacy, it's fitting that this city should be the home of an enlightening museum devoted to Scotland's firefighting heritage and the selfless individuals, past and present, who have committed their lives to this vital public service. The gallery, next to a working fire station, isn't vast, but the well-designed displays contain a huge amount of intriguing information, with user-friendly digital interactives as well as a fascinating selection of artefacts and vehicles from the Fire and Rescue Service's collection of more than 10,000 items. The magnificent vintage engines are of course an immediate draw, but you'll also learn about topics as diverse as fire insurance plaques, the evolution of helmets and boots, and the contribution made by specially trained dogs. What gives immediacy to the exhibits is the presence of retired firefighters as guides, on hand to deepen your understanding through their first-hand knowledge and make your visit a truly memorable and humbling experience.

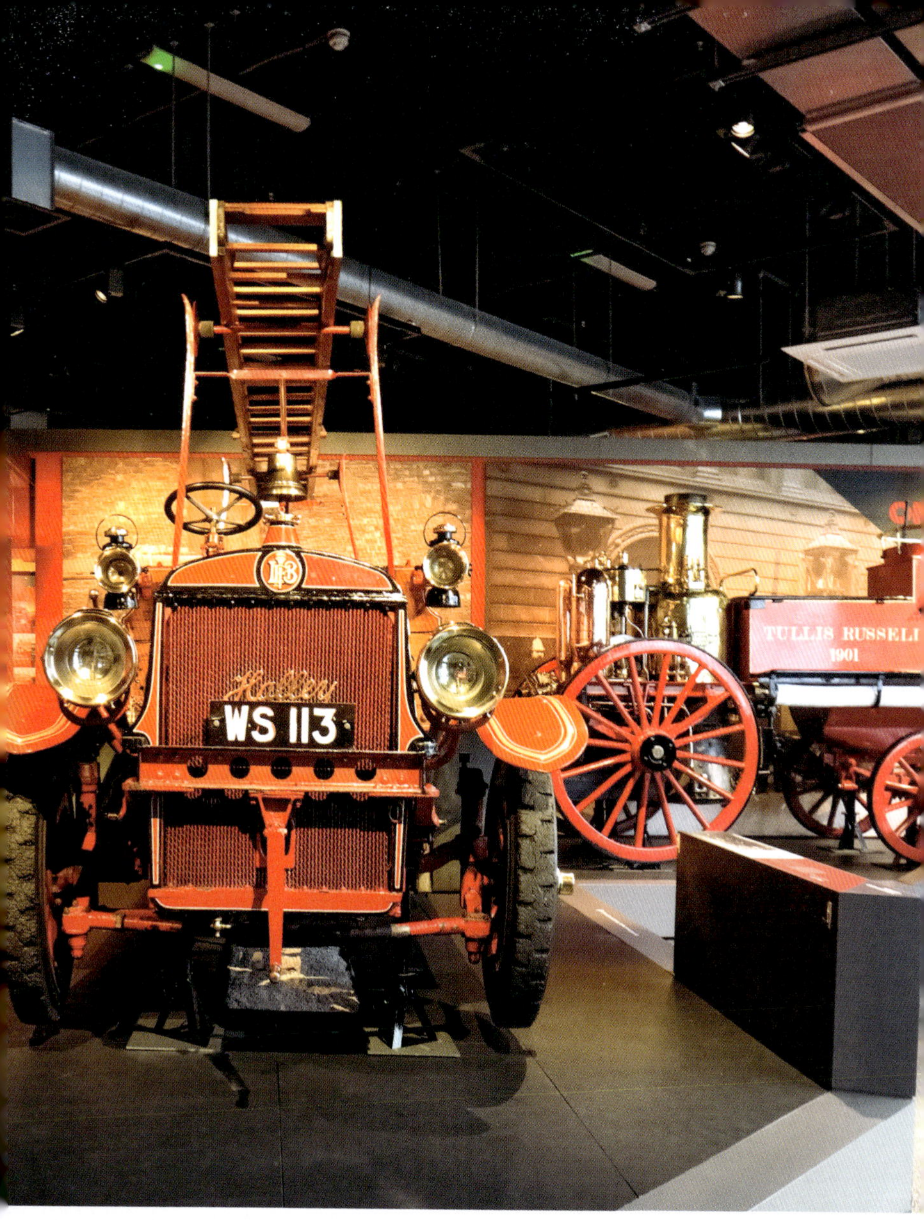

Address 1A Dryden Terrace, EH7 4NB, +44 (0)131 550 4954, www.museumofscottishfireheritage.org | Getting there Lothian Buses 10 to McDonald Road (Hopetoun Crescent) or 11, 14, 16, 25, 36 or 49 to Leith Walk (Shrubhill); Tram to McDonald Road | Hours Tue–Sat 10am–4pm | Tip A bronze statue of James Braidwood, the founder of modern firefighting techniques, stands in Parliament Square on the Royal Mile. The work of Kenny Mackay, a former assistant of Sandy Stoddart, it was commissioned after a public fundraising campaign, and unveiled in 2008 at a ceremony attended by firefighters in historic uniform, accompanied by horse-drawn vintage fire engines.

68 The Museum on the Mound

Money matters

Although the reputation of the Scots as prudent and reliable bankers has taken a hammering in recent years, the capital's long and proud history as a financial centre remains unassailable. In other world cities, a splendidly prominent site like that of the Bank of Scotland's huge head office would probably have been allocated to the State or the Church, but in Edinburgh it doesn't seem so surprising that it's the home of a monument to money and its management.

Scotland's oldest bank was established in 1695 – just a year after the Bank of England was founded (by the Scot William Paterson). When new headquarters were needed a century later, a prime location was cleverly chosen, overlooking the emergent New Town, at the top of what was then known as the Earthen Mound. The nature of the site created engineering problems, and the original building was rather grim, but in 1864 it was totally remodelled in handsome Italianate style by the capable David Bryce, who added a conspicuous dome crowned with a two-metre gilded statue of Victory.

Most of the magnificent interior is now closed to the public. The basement, however, houses a little museum devoted to the history of the building, the bank, and money in general, which manages to make potentially dull subjects genuinely entertaining. It tackles topics such as forgery and safe-cracking, and illustrates the social history behind life assurance and building societies. Original currency on show ranges from gorgeous Melanesian red feather money to a dour Scottish banknote from 1716. You can look at a million pounds in wads of the Bank's own notes – all bearing the image of Sir Walter Scott, who in 1826 successfully campaigned against the UK government's attempt to interfere with Scotland's paper currency. Later, an irresistible display allows you to see how you would look emblazoned in his place.

Address The Mound, EH1 1YZ, +44 (0)131 243 5464, www.museumonthemound.com | Getting there Lothian Buses 9, 23 or 27 to the foot of the Mound, or walk up from Princes Street | Hours Tue–Fri 10am–5pm, Sat & Bank Holiday Mon 1–5pm | Tip Opposite the museum entrance on Market Street, the Playfair Steps lead down to the National Gallery of Scotland and its magnificent collections. Its popular Scottish Café and Restaurant serves breakfast, lunch, and afternoon tea (daily 10am–5pm).

69 The National Monument

A magnificent disgrace

Of all the stunning sights that animate the city centre skyline, perhaps the most remarkable is the silhouette on Calton Hill of what appears to be a ruined Greek temple. This classical fragment is a war memorial, officially called the National Monument, but to those who still remember something of its story, it's better known as 'Edinburgh's Disgrace'.

A memorial to the Scots who had died in the hard-fought Napoleonic Wars was first mooted in 1815; after several years' discussion it was agreed that this should be a grand church which, as part of the capital's aspiration to reinvent itself as a 'Modern Athens', would take the form of an exact copy of the Parthenon. There was widespread enthusiasm for the wildly ambitious scheme, though unfortunately this didn't translate into hard cash. The estimated cost was £42,000, but much less than half of this had actually been raised when construction began in 1826, and it soon became clear that even that target figure was grossly inadequate. It took 12 horses and 70 men to move each of the massive sandstone blocks, some of the largest ever to be cut from Craigleith Quarry, and the architect Playfair's insistence on a standard of workmanship that the ancient Greeks would have admired also came at a price. Money ran out after 3 years, with only 12 columns erected, and it wasn't long before the 'folly' was denigrated as an embarrassment to the city.

The truth is that there probably never was a realistic intention to build more than the small section that was finished. An entire Parthenon replica would have measured a vast 70 by 30 metres, and required a total of 69 colossal columns. Unsurprisingly, subsequent proposals for the monument's completion – as a new national gallery, among other things – have come to nothing, which is just as well, as Edinburgh folk have grown fond of it as it is, disgraceful or not.

Address Calton Hill, EH7 5AA | Getting there Lothian Buses 15, 26, X26, 43, 44, X44, 113 or 124 to Regent Road (St Andrew's House), then take the flight of steps up the hill (an unexpectedly easy climb!) | Tip Calton Hill is home to other unusual buildings, including the telescope-like Nelson Monument, which has a viewing platform at the top. Look out for the ball on its mast, which drops down at 1pm every day except Sunday – originally as a time signal for ships in the port of Leith (daily 10am–1pm & 2–5pm).

70_Newhailes

Original splendour – unrestored

A visit to the grand villa of Newhailes is a refreshingly unusual experience. It's far from being yet another sanitised stately home 'restored to its original splendour' and frozen at an arbitrary stage in its past. This is a historic house that has been allowed to maintain a unique character acquired over three centuries, and to continue growing old gracefully.

For most of its life the late 17th-century house and its estate were, exceptionally, the home of a single dynasty. It was bought in 1709 as a rural retreat by Sir David Dalrymple, a prosperous lawyer and MP, and it was the widow of the last of his line, Lady Antonia Dalrymple, who in 1997 handed it into the care of conservation charity the National Trust for Scotland. The Trust had previously been criticised for its over-zealous approach to the renovation of historic buildings, but in the late 1990s a combination of financial belt-tightening and new thinking in line with more conservative approaches elsewhere led to a change in policy. So it was that Newhailes became the first of its properties to be 'conserved as found'.

The house's special ambience strikes you as soon as you enter, and helps the well-informed guides to paint memorable pictures of its inhabitants – for the moment, you actually feel you're sharing in their lives of intellectual pursuit and sophisticated enjoyment. Much of the interior decor – paint finishes, decorative plasterwork, and even wallpaper – survives virtually intact from the 18th century, and fine portraits by the likes of Allan Ramsay are set into the panelling. Though now sadly bereft of its books, the library still evokes its time as 'the most learned drawing room in Europe'. The only jarring note for today's visitors is the glimpse of life below stairs, in particular the access tunnel to the house, where your visit ends. This was built to keep the servants' comings and goings out of the sight and hearing of their superiors.

Address Newhailes Road, EH21 6RY, +44 (0)131 653 5599, www.nts.org/visit/places/newhailes | Getting there Lothian Buses 30 to Newhailes Road (Newhailes NTS) | Hours House: pre-booked tours only; Jan & Feb Thu–Sun, Mar–Oct daily, from 11am | Tip The nearby historic seaside town of Musselburgh is home to Luca's café, established in 1908 and long famed throughout the Lothians for its real Italian ice cream (32–38 High Street, Musselburgh, EH21 7AG, daily 9am–10pm).

71_The Oily Well

Liberton's healing balm

Half-hidden in the grass outside an unremarkable roadhouse on the city's southern fringe sits a curious little well, once widely venerated as a source of healing, but long ignored. For centuries, paupers and royalty alike knelt here to gather its sacred – and decidedly pungent – waters; now only urban foxes swagger around the unkempt site.

Everyone knows that oil and water don't mix, and springs where both elements bubble up out of the ground together used to be held in awe. The tarry content of Liberton's Oily Well, which coats its tiny vaulted interior, led to its association in medieval times with the early Christian martyr who was tortured on the wheel, St Catherine of Alexandria. An ancient legend claimed that a flow of holy oil exuded from her burial place on Mount Sinai, and according to tradition, the spring at Liberton arose when a phial of this oil belonging to the devout Queen Margaret of Scotland was accidentally spilt there.

The well became celebrated for its curative properties, particularly for skin complaints; its water was commonly held to heal 'all scabs and humours that trouble the outward skin of man'. In the 16th century King James IV was a regular patron, as well as princes and diplomats from as far afield as Denmark and Pomerania, who collected samples to take home. A stone well-house was built in 1617 by order of James VI, though this was later vandalised by Cromwell's army, and what is visible today is an odd affair cobbled together in the 19th century.

By then it was known that the spring's oily character came from bituminous shale deposits in the rocks, but this didn't make the well any less popular, and it was still in use by locals up to a century ago. In fact, there is good reason to think that its healing properties were quite genuine: coal tar is still prescribed today as an effective, if smelly treatment for eczema and psoriasis.

Address 41 Howden Hall Road, EH16 6PG; in the grounds of the Toby Carvery, near the car park | **Getting there** Lothian Buses 7, 37, 47 or 47A to Howden Hall Road (Mortonhall) | **Tip** Seven Acre Park is a refreshing green space less than a mile away, sited on former farmland just south of the Braid Hills. As well as picnic tables, woodland, and extensive children's play facilities, it has superb views of the city skyline and beyond, taking in Arthur's Seat, Salisbury Crags and Edinburgh Castle (Stanedykehead, Alnwickhill, EH16 6TN).

72_Old College

Triumphal gateway to knowledge

Edinburgh University was established in 1583 by decree of James VI, on the site of Kirk o' Field, the scene 16 years earlier of the murder of Lord Darnley, consort of his mother, Mary, Queen of Scots. The distinguished seat of learning occupied an increasingly dilapidated jumble of buildings for over two centuries, until funds were finally raised to construct a custom-built college in their place.

The neoclassical architect Robert Adam was given the brief, and produced a fittingly grandiose scheme. Construction began in 1789, but work stopped in 1793 after Adam's death, with only the entrance gateway completed. It's still an awe-inspiring achievement, as impressive as a real Roman triumphal arch, with 6 columns over 6 metres high, each cut out of a single piece of stone. However, its position, hemmed in on busy South Bridge, makes it difficult now to appreciate anything except the dome, which was added a century later and is much larger than Adam intended.

The massive scale of the gateway also tends to daunt casual visitors, though those who do venture through its portals find themselves in a quadrangle that is one of the most attractive open spaces in the city centre. This was the work of William Playfair, who took over the building project in 1819; it suffered decades of misuse as a car park before being sympathetically remodelled in 2011. Playfair also created some splendid interiors; sadly, his magnificent Upper Library is rarely open to the public, but the handsome Museum Hall, where Charles Darwin studied natural history specimens, is now part of the Talbot Rice Gallery, a contemporary art venue.

An archaeological dig prior to the quad's restoration unearthed fascinating finds, including a laboratory used by the influential 18th-century chemist Joseph Black. The site of Darnley's assassination was also uncovered – but without any helpful clues to solve the mystery of 'whodunnit'.

Address University of Edinburgh, South Bridge, EH8 9YL, +44 (0)131 650 1000, www.ed.ac.uk | Getting there Lothian Buses 3, 5, 7, 8, 14, 29, 30, 31, 33, 35, 37, 45 or 49 to South Bridge | Hours Quadrangle: 8am–9.30pm; Talbot Rice Gallery: Tue–Sat 10am–5pm | Tip Just across the road is Blackwell's, Edinburgh' oldest bookshop, with an exceptional selection of around 250,000 titles spread over three expansive floors. Established in 1848 by James Thin, it remained in the same family for five generations, becoming a renowned stockist of academic textbooks and a much-loved Edinburgh institution. Though the business was sold in 2002, many older locals still refer to it as Thin's.

73 The Old Royal High School

The parliament that never was

The building that most justifies the city's claim to be the 'Athens of the North' is the Greek Revival temple completed in 1829 for the Royal High School. Dramatically sited on Calton Hill, it was designed by architect Thomas Hamilton to be a major element of what was intended as Edinburgh's Acropolis. However, since the school vacated it in 1969, this noble structure has had mixed fortunes. It has now lain neglected for decades, the object of lamentable ill-treatment by the city which once viewed it with legitimate pride.

An egalitarian institution, offering a classical education to all (male) children, the High School was founded around 1128, and taken over by the Town Council in 1566. In the 1820s the city fathers decided that a new building was needed, to compete with the privatised Edinburgh Academy, and Hamilton was commissioned to design a monument fitting to the ideals of the Scottish Enlightenment, which he based on the Temple of Theseus in Athens.

The school eventually moved out to larger modern premises; nearly a decade later, during the lead-up to the 1979 referendum on devolution, the unused building was proposed as a home for the anticipated new Scottish Assembly, and work began on a debating chamber. In the event, the vote in favour was insufficient, and the Calton Hill site then became a symbol of the campaign for independence. But when devolution finally became a reality two decades later, what would have made a fine parliament house was spurned in favour of a pricy new-build option at Holyrood.

The good news is that after a long period of uncertainty, the fate of the building has finally been resolved. Following the rejection of a controversial proposal to convert it into a luxury hotel, and many false starts, it was announced in January 2025 that funding was at last in place to develop it into a National Centre for Music. The muses will find a fitting home in this temple.

Address 5–7 Regent Road, EH7 5BL | Getting there Lothian Buses 15, 26, X26, 44, X44, 113 or 124 to Regent Road | Hours Currently viewable from the outside only | Tip One of the major backers of the Royal High School project, the Dunard Fund, is also behind the construction of an exciting new world-class concert hall, due to open in 2029 on a site just off St Andrew Square, behind Dundas House (see ch. 32).

74_ The Oxford Bar

Inspector Rebus' no-nonsense boozer

It's far from clear why the Oxford Bar is so called – there's no apparent connection between this unreconstructed old Edinburgh pub in a New Town back lane and the prestigious English university town of dreaming spires. But whatever you do, don't confuse it with the Cambridge Bar along the road, which boasts gourmet burgers, wide-screen sports TV, and quiz nights. You won't find any of that nonsense at 'the Ox'.

Said to be the least altered pub in Edinburgh, the Oxford Bar is still much as it was in the late 19th century. It's one of the few in the city which hasn't been fitted with large windows, so it remains a discreet den for drinking and conversation, the latter of which will almost inevitably involve the bar staff. It gained worldwide fame through the writing of Ian Rankin, as the regular haunt of his Inspector Rebus, though fans who call in expecting some sort of tribute or theme pub will be rather disappointed. The place has only two modest, worn and homely rooms, with wooden pews for seating in the snug at the back, and a real fire in winter.

Rankin discovered it in his student days when he was working on his first Rebus novel, and the author still drops by for the occasional pint. But the Ox's literary credentials predate his hardboiled fictional policeman. In the mid-20th century, under the legendary licensee Willie Ross – known for refusing to serve women, Englishmen, or food – it was often favoured by writers of the so-called Scottish Renaissance, such as Sydney Goodsir Smith, who immortalised it in Joycean style as 'Wullie Roose's Coxfork in Bung Strait'.

The nicknames now extend to various areas of the bar – newcomers tend to occupy the 'Visitors' Paddock', the Friday night scrum congregates in the 'Carousel', and 'Dead Man's Corner' is by the extractor fan. Things have never changed much at the Ox, and long may they stay that way.

Address 8 Young Street, EH2 4JB, +44 (0)131 539 7119 | Getting there Lothian Buses 24 or 29 to Frederick Street (Hill Street); Hill Street leads into Young Street | Hours Mon–Thu 11am–midnight, Fri & Sat 11am–1am, Sun 12.30–11pm | Tip A rather grander nearby building with literary credentials is 17 Heriot Row, childhood home of Robert Louis Stevenson. Its current owners have two rooms to let for bed and breakfast (www.stevenson-house.com).

75 Parliament Square

Historic hub of genius and learning

The elegant space that flanks St Giles' Cathedral has all the elements of a fine city-centre piazza – historical surroundings, covered arcades, even an equestrian statue. Yet Parliament Square today is a lifeless place, its barren asphalt deserted apart from a few privileged cars and an occasional advocate bustling to court. It's difficult to believe that in the golden age of the 18th century, when the city was famed as an intellectual powerhouse, this area was Edinburgh's busiest hub, a place where an English visitor declared he could 'take fifty men of genius and learning by the hand' within a few minutes. Everyone congregated here to meet, talk, or do business – judges, philosophers, poets, and politicians sharing space with ministers, merchants, hawkers and idlers.

Most of the public affairs of the city used to be carried on inside the surrounding buildings. Parliament House, the seat of Scottish government until 1707, was built in the 1630s opposite the city's principal church, with a grand 36.5-metre hall and magnificent hammerbeam roof. The Supreme Court shared its premises, and in later centuries the legal profession gradually took over much of the square. Market stalls, as well as shops known as luckenbooths once ringed the whole area. There were goldsmiths, and booksellers, where the *literati* gathered. The Mercat Cross, at the east end, was the meeting place for merchants, and for 'caddies', the town's indispensable guides and messengers. Near St Giles' west end was the medieval Tolbooth, a notorious jail, long gone but remembered by a heart shape in the pavement, still spat on by some Edinburgh folk as a sign of contempt.

The statue of Charles II on horseback, cast in lead, is the work of Grinling Gibbons, and was erected in 1685. The famously merry monarch looks rather uncomfortable in his guise as Caesar – and distinctly lonely, now that he so rarely has any company.

Address Parliament Square, EH1 1RF; off the High Street | Getting there Lothian Buses 9, 23 or 27 to George IV Bridge (National Library) | Hours Parliament Hall (entrance at Court of Session, 11 Parliament Square): Mon–Fri 10am–4pm | Tip Colonnades, a luxurious afternoon tea salon, operates within the elegant and historic Signet Library, on the south side of the square. Drinks and light lunches are also served (Wed–Sun 11am–4.30pm).

76 The People's Story

Vintage scenes from ordinary lives

A new museum celebrating Edinburgh's working-class heritage was a radical proposal when it was first mooted in 1984 – and a timely change of direction for a city whose public image had always flagged its upper-echelon status and refined cultural milieu. Opened five years later in the characterful old Canongate Tolbooth, its name, The People's Story, reflects the equally radical methodology used in its creation: thanks to pioneering curator and oral historian Helen Clark, the museum took its inspiration from the reminiscences of ordinary Edinburgh folk talking about their own lived experience, at work and at play, together with first-hand written accounts from more distant times.

The displays take the visitor from the late 18th to the late 20th century, with historic artefacts and information panels complemented by tableaux featuring life-sized mannequins based on real individuals – a fishwife, a tram conductress, a domestic servant, a cooper and a bookbinder, among others, represented alongside the tools of their trade. You'll also see 18th-century prisoners languishing in the (genuine) tolbooth cell, two housewives of the 1930s chatting in a tearoom while their husbands drink in a nearby pub, and 1980s youngsters out on the razzle.

Themes covered include trade unions and the fight for political rights, crime and punishment, poverty, housing and homelessness as well as sport, religion and community festivals. The contribution of women in the workplace, so often marginalised, is given due prominence, with recognition of the key rôles they once played in numerous industries, from the printing trade to whisky production.

In the autumn of 2024, news emerged that the city council planned to 'mothball' the museum as a cost-cutting measure, but after a public outcry this unpopular decision was hastily reversed, and it's now open daily throughout the year.

Address 163 Canongate, EH8 8BN, +44 (0)131 529 4057, www.edinburghmuseums.org.uk/venue/peoples-story-museum | Getting there Lothian Buses 35 to Canongate Kirk | Hours Daily 10am–5pm | Tip Just across the road is Huntly House, the rambling 16th-century mansion that forms the home of the Museum of Edinburgh. Its wide-ranging collections include decorative arts, rare documents and a host of intriguing objects that complement the displays of the People's Story in presenting the history of the capital.

77_Piershill Cemetery

The sensational last act of a celebrity dog lover

If the illusionist Sigmund Neuberger possessed any real psychic faculties, he must have felt a sense of foreboding when he laid his beloved dog to rest at Piershill Cemetery in May 1911. Neuberger, internationally famed as 'The Great Lafayette', was in the middle of a sell-out run at the city's Empire Theatre. He was an A-list celebrity, one of the highest paid performers in the world, renowned for his elaborately staged illusions, which involved quick-change routines, glamorous assistants, and a small menagerie of animals. His favourite of these by far was his pampered terrier Beauty, given to him by his friend Houdini.

When Beauty died suddenly during his Edinburgh season, Lafayette insisted on giving her a proper burial in a city cemetery. Such a thing was unheard of, but the authorities finally agreed to let him buy a plot at Piershill, on condition that it would also, eventually, contain his own remains, wherever and whenever he died.

The following Tuesday, a rapt theatre audience of 3,000 were watching Lafayette perform his grand finale 'The Lion's Bride' when tragedy struck. A lamp fused and set fire to the scenery, and the ensuing conflagration claimed the lives of 11 people, including the great illusionist himself. Five days later, his ashes were placed between the paws of his canine friend, in her coffin at Piershill, after the most extravagantly showy funeral the city had ever seen. The cortège was led by his chief mourner, a Dalmatian, riding in Lafayette's Mercedes.

In 1967, Beauty's final resting place became the site of Scotland's first pet cemetery, when the owner of Captain, a German Shepherd, endowed a section of Piershill for animal burials. More than 2,000 faithful companions were interred here before it was closed in 2002, and the loving inscriptions on their tiny headstones are genuinely touching. The Great Lafayette would surely have approved.

Address 204 Piersfield Terrace, Portobello Road, EH8 7BN | Getting there Lothian Buses 15, 21, 26 or 45 to Portobello Road (Craigentinny Avenue) | Hours Daily 9am–6pm (4pm during winter months) | Tip The Dog Cemetery at Edinburgh Castle has been used since the 1840s as a graveyard for regimental mascots and soldiers' pets. Though not accessible to the public, it can viewed from above at Mill's Mount, the site of the One O'Clock Gun.

78 The Political Martyrs' Monument

The cause of the people

The 27-metre-tall obelisk in the burial ground on Calton Hill is a conspicuous Edinburgh monument. But although a crowd of 3,000 gathered to celebrate its dedication in 1844, few citizens today, let alone visitors, have any idea what it stands for. The reason is simple: in the mid-19th century the cause that it represented was still a burning issue. Now it's a battle long since won.

The monument, designed by architect Thomas Hamilton, was erected to commemorate the five men known as the Scottish Political Martyrs, who had been sentenced to transportation to New South Wales in 1793 and 1794. Their crime was to promote the right of all male citizens, regardless of wealth, social rank or education, to vote in parliamentary elections. The British ruling classes of the time were extremely nervous about the spread across the Channel of the revolutionary ideas that had led to the overthrow of the French monarchy, and they cracked down severely on anyone believed to be stirring discontent among the masses. Five key campaigners for political reform – Thomas Muir, Thomas Fyshe Palmer, William Skirving, Maurice Margarot and Joseph Gerrald – were tried in Edinburgh, convicted of sedition and transported. Though Muir escaped to France in 1796, he and all the others died prematurely, mostly from diseases caught in Australia.

Inscribed on the obelisk are some prophetic words from a speech Muir made at his trial: 'I have devoted myself to the cause of the people. It is a good cause – it shall ultimately prevail.' In fact it was not until 1918 that universal suffrage (including limited voting rights for women) was introduced in the UK. It is a sobering experience to stand at the foot of this pillar reaching for the sky, and reflect that a right we now take for granted was once the dream of heroes.

Address Old Calton Burial Ground, 26 Waterloo Place, EH1 3BQ | Getting there Lothian Buses X26, 43, X44, 113 or 124 to Waterloo Place | Hours Daily 8am–dusk | Tip In the same cemetery is a bronze statue of Abraham Lincoln, the first monument to an American president to be erected outside the USA. It was dedicated in 1893 to the memory of the Scottish troops who fought and died in the American Civil War.

79 The Portobello Pottery Kilns

Days of ginger beer and hot water bottles

Though now a largely residential suburb of the capital, the coastal town of Portobello has its own character, and a uniquely diverse history. During its long heyday as a seaside resort it was also a major manufacturing centre, and the pleasure beach coexisted with three brickworks and two potteries, a paper mill, and factories producing glassware, lead, soap and mustard.

The town has recently preserved an important monument to one of its earliest and most enduring industries – pottery production. This had its beginnings in the 1770s, when the entrepreneur William Jamieson began to exploit a bed of clay near the Figgate Burn, soon expanding his original manufacture of bricks and tiles to include ceramics. The success of these businesses led to the construction of workers' cottages, which formed the nucleus of the village that became Portobello.

Now awkwardly marooned behind a bland seafront housing development, two huge brick kilns still stand on their original site, the sole survivors in the whole of Scotland of what was once an important industry across the Central Belt. These defiantly prominent structures are the last remains of A. W. Buchan & Co.'s Thistle Pottery, which flourished for over a century before its closure in 1972. It was primarily famed for its high quality, durable stoneware, which mostly took the form of bottles – stone-stoppered ones for ginger beer, demijohns for whisky, and hot water 'pigs' for warming cold beds, among many other lines.

The kilns are of a type called updraught ovens, but they're better known as 'bottle kilns' – because of their distinctive shape rather than the products they so often fired. The Portobello pair, which date from 1906 and 1909, were rescued from dereliction thanks to the local Heritage Trust, and their restoration was completed in 2014.

Address Bridge Street, Portobello, EH15 1DB | **Getting there** Lothian Buses 12, 19, 21, 26, 45 or 49 to Portobello High Street (Bridge Street) | **Tip** Five minutes' walk away along the Promenade is the Beach House, a licensed café open for breakfast, lunch, supper and takeaway, with an imaginative menu based where possible on organic, locally sourced ingredients. Their home-made cakes and ice-cream are particularly popular (57 Bath Street, EH15 1HE; www.thebeachhousecafe.co.uk).

80_Portobello Promenade

We do like to be beside the seaside

When trips to sun-kissed foreign shores were dreams way beyond the reach of the masses, Edinburgh folk flocked to 'Porty' for their holidays. Fashionable urban dwellers started visiting the seaside at Portobello, just three miles east of the city centre, at the end of the 18th century, dipping into the chilly water from discreet bathing machines. Many rented houses for the summer in what was Scotland's only planned Regency spa town. In the Victorian era, trippers of all social classes came down by rail, in carriages first drawn by horses and later driven by steam.

The promenade along the shore was built in 1876, and other attractions soon sprang up nearby: a pier with a large pavilion, a funfair, and both indoor and outdoor swimming pools, the latter heated by steam from the nearby power station. The young Sean Connery worked there as a lifeguard in the early 1950s, gaining valuable experience for the aquatic sequences that were a feature of his early Bond films.

The name Portobello dates from a time when this region was a barren heath. The story goes that a cottage built here in the 1750s was named after the Battle of Puerto Bello in Panama by a retired sailor, George Hamilton, who had seen action there. The rather exotic name stuck, though the site was neither a port nor a place of conventional beauty.

Most of the traditional holiday facilities are long gone, though there are plans to reinstate the pier. Where a bandstand once stood on the promenade, there is now a quiet little garden with three intricately decorated pillars, from one of the Georgian villas that used to grace the town. Their pristine condition is due to the fact that they were cast from hard-wearing Coade stone, a fired ceramic incorporating ground flint, invented by 18th-century entrepreneur Mrs Eleanor Coade. They are an elegant reminder of the past glories of this atmospheric resort.

Address Portobello, EH15 2DX; the Promenade runs along the shore, parallel to the High Street | **Getting there** Lothian Buses 12, 19, 21, 26, 45 or 49 to Portobello High Street | **Tip** If the weather isn't quite Mediterranean, you'll feel the benefit of a visit to the Victorian Turkish baths, one of the last remaining in Scotland, at the nearby Portobello Swim Centre (57 The Promenade; open daily, check www.edinburghleisure.co.uk for hours).

81_The Portrait Gallery Entrance Hall

Gilded heroes of the nation

Public galleries devoted to images of the nation's famous sons and daughters are an institution beloved of English-speaking countries, found only in the capital cities of Scotland, England, the USA, Australia and Canada. The Scottish National Portrait Gallery was established in 1882, though the UK government was reluctant to fund the project, and when the growing collection was moved into grand new premises in 1890, it was entirely thanks to the generous sponsorship of local newspaper proprietor J. R. Findlay, who commissioned the architect Robert Rowand Anderson to design what was the first purpose-built portrait gallery in the world.

Together they created a fitting neo-Gothic shrine for Scotland's heroes – a sort of palace-cum-cathedral, which creates an impression that's both richly resplendent and massively imposing. The striking red sandstone building proudly proclaims its function with statues of luminaries in niches around the outside, including William Wallace and Robert the Bruce, who flank the main entrance.

But the real jewel in the crown is just inside the door. The first sight of the double-storeyed central hall – justifiably dubbed Scotland's Valhalla – often inspires an involuntary reverential hush. By the soft light of wrought-iron hanging lanterns, a gorgeous procession unfolds around the gallery above, as almost 150 Scottish historical figures, from ancient times up to the Victorian era, line up elegantly against the gleaming gold background. This dazzling pageant was the work of the Edinburgh-trained William Hole, an estimable craftsman who also painted the tapestry-like scenes on the first floor balcony, and the celestial ceiling, decorated with 2,222 golden stars arranged in constellations. The whole scheme was cleaned in 2011 as part of the gallery's major overhaul.

Address Scottish National Portrait Gallery, 1 Queen Street, EH2 1JD, +44 (0)131 624 6200, www.nationalgalleries.org | **Getting there** Lothian Buses 10 or 11 to Queen Street, or Tram to St Andrew Square | **Hours** Daily 10am–5pm | **Tip** The stylish Forth Floor Restaurant in Harvey Nichols' nearby department store has an outdoor terrace, with expansive views over city rooftops – including the Portrait Gallery's – out to the Firth of Forth (open daily).

82_The Radical Road

A walk for romantics, built by revolutionaries

The park of Holyrood is one of the most exceptional open spaces within any city in the world. At its heart is a mountain wilderness, with the rugged slopes of Arthur's Seat (more like a frozen mammoth than the crouching lion that it traditionally resembles) flanked by the skewed frieze of massive angular pillars that make up Salisbury Crags. Yet this wild country is easily accessible, and the highly scenic walk around the base of the Crags is little more than a gentle stroll, along the path known as the Radical Road.

This was originally a rough, ill-defined track, used from early times by quarrymen extracting hard, volcanic dolerite – in demand for street paving as far afield as London – from the Crags' cliff-face. In the late 18th century, these rocks became the object of study by the pioneering geologist James Hutton, who used his observations in the South Quarry to prove his revolutionary theory that they had formed out of molten material from beneath the Earth's crust.

Quarrying operations gained momentum at the turn of the 19th century, after explosives began to be used, and soon the Crags' profile was visibly eroded. In 1819, the Keeper of the Park, Lord Haddington, was officially called upon to stop removing – and selling – the stone, though it was 12 more years before the destruction finally ceased. Meanwhile, the path skirting the Crags was paved and improved, for recreational use. In 1820, thanks to a committee headed by the writer Walter Scott, this work was given to unemployed weavers from the west of Scotland who had been involved in the week of civil unrest known as the Radical War. The hard labour was intended to rid these master craftsmen of their insurrectionist ideas. For generations afterwards, they were mocked by Edinburgh children in the tongue-twisting chant 'Round and round the Radical Road the Radical rascal ran…'

Address Holyrood Park, EH16 | Getting there Lothian Buses 2, 14, 30 or 33 to Dalkeith Road (Commonwealth Pool), then walk down Holyrood Park Road to the park entrance. The south end of the Radical Road is straight ahead, just off Queen's Drive. | Hours The Radical Road has been closed in recent years owing to rockfalls, but public access is due to be restored in spring 2025. | Tip There are numerous other rewarding hikes to be had within the park. The ascent to Arthur's Seat has now become almost too popular, but a much less busy alternative is the crag of Dunsapie, above the pleasant artificial loch of the same name, which can be accessed via the steep grassy slope to the east. At 145 metres above sea level, it offers superb views over East Lothian.

83 Ramsay Garden

Castles in the air

When the poet Hugh MacDiarmid characterised Edinburgh as 'a mad god's dream', one of the images he had in mind must surely have been the wildly romantic view from Princes Street of the Old Town ridge, with its extraordinary cascade of battlements, turrets, domes and spires.

Just below the Castle Esplanade, there is one exceptionally eccentric cluster that seems to soar above the trees of Princes Street Gardens – the enclave of Ramsay Garden which, with its red and white gables and conical towers, looks beguilingly like a cross between a fairytale baron's castle and a medieval English village.

This rambling confection was conceived in the early 1890s by the utopian visionary Patrick Geddes – the father of modern town planning – as part of his move to halt the decline of the Old Town. Ramsay Garden is actually a five-storey block of spacious flats, built as a town-and-gown residence to attract university academics away from classier New Town addresses. Geddes dreamt of recreating the spirit of the city's 18th century Golden Age, when all its great thinkers lived and met up around the Royal Mile. At the heart of the block there is in fact a distinguished building that dates from this period – the octagonal 'Goose Pie House' built for the poet Allan Ramsay, father of the portraitist.

Geddes himself lived with his family in a 12-room apartment within the complex he called 'the seven-towered castle I built for my beloved'. On the roof of the wing he used to occupy there is a large figure of a feline creature with an upturned tail. It once had wings, and originally formed part of a lost trio of angel, demon and sphinx, arranged like Chinese temple effigies, and apparently signifying the riddle of life. In old age, Geddes' daughter Norah identified the surviving cat as the demon, though it seems rather more likely to be a particularly agile sphinx.

Address Ramsay Garden, EH1 2NA | Getting there Lothian Buses 9, 23 or 27 to the Foot of the Mound, then walk uphill via Ramsay Lane – the 'cat' is best seen from there | Hours Viewable from the outside only (though some flats may be available as holiday lets) | Tip Among Geddes' initiatives was the creation of a network of children's gardens on derelict sites in the Old Town, a scheme carried out under the capable direction of his daughter Norah. Several of these have now been restored, most notably the West Port Garden, a splendid community initiative at the southwest end of the Grassmarket (open Sun 2–4pm).

84 Real Foods

The principle of natural selection

Thank goodness for Real Foods – one retailer whose name actually means what it says. When they set up shop in the city five decades ago, the truth about the food we eat didn't seem such a pressing issue to most people. Now, in an environment almost overwhelmed by cloned supermarkets filled with industrially processed fare, an independent store where terms like 'natural' and 'fresh' are not just cynical marketing jargon is a positive godsend.

Real Foods was one of the UK's first wholefood businesses, founded in the days when such things were considered cranky, if not downright subversive. Its origins go back to 1963, and a stall selling organic vegetables in a London market.

The company later branched out into importing macrobiotic ingredients, and in 1975 it took over a store in Edinburgh's Broughton Street, originally as a warehouse for its mail order business. That soon became a shop, and in 1981 a second branch was opened at Tollcross. Most of its grains and pulses were sold loose, out of large sacks, as many still are today. At a time when the city still had at least one traditional 'victual dealer' (the fondly remembered Robert Thomson's), this was not a novelty, but virtually everything else about the Real Foods philosophy was refreshingly radical.

Today, it still leads the field in natural, healthy, ethical shopping in Edinburgh and, through its website, way beyond. Its two city stores are stocked with a huge range of over 10,000 lines – fruit and vegetables, organic and locally sourced where possible, and a massive variety of grocery staples and specialist items, as well as herbal remedies, natural cosmetics and cleaning products. The dedicated staff can advise on cooking methods and dietary problems, and help you find your quinoa crispbread, kelp noodles, smoked tofu, or 'superfoods' like oats and kale – both of which Scots have known about for generations, by the way.

Address 8 Brougham Street, EH3 9JH, +44 (0)131 228 1201, also at 37 Broughton Street, EH1 3JU, www.realfoods.co.uk | Getting there Lothian Buses 10, 11, 15, 16, 23, 24, 27, 36 or 45 to Tollcross | Hours Mon–Fri 9am–7pm, Sat 9am–6pm, Sun 10am–5pm | Tip There are two, more recently established wholefood businesses in the vicinity that are also well worth seeking out – The New Leaf Co-op at 23 Argyle Place, EH9 1JJ (www.newleafcoop.co.uk) and Dig-in Community Greengrocer at 119 Bruntsfield Place, EH10 4EQ (www.diginbruntsfield.co.uk).

85_The Robin Chapel

Music and praise in perpetuity

Although urban regeneration is now underway in Craigmillar, its reputation as a district blighted by social deprivation still lingers. It's not a place where many Edinburgh people or indeed tourists would normally think of going to enjoy exquisite music in a lovely ecclesiastical setting, and so, though its weekly choral services are open to all, the unique haven of peace that is the Robin Chapel remains a little-visited secret.

The Robin Chapel was completed in 1953 at the centre of the Thistle Foundation, a housing complex for disabled veterans of World War II and their families. The inscription above its entrance begins 'Come in, come in…', and the chapel welcomes everyone, regardless of denomination, to its choral evensong each Sunday afternoon throughout the year. Prayers and sacred music by the likes of Byrd, Elgar, and Parry are sung to organ accompaniment by the fine professional choir and chaplain – whether or not there is a congregation to hear them.

The Thistle Foundation was the charitable project of Sir Francis and Lady Tudsbery, wealthy aristocrats with an estate near Linlithgow. Planning had already begun when in May 1945 they received news that their 25-year-old only child Robin had been blown up by a mine in the final days of the war. In their grief at his tragic loss, the Tudsberys decided to incorporate a chapel into the complex as a shrine to his memory, and to provide an endowment for services to be held in perpetuity.

The foundation stone was laid in 1950 by the then Queen Elizabeth; Robin had served for nine months as bodyguard to her daughter, the present queen. The light and airy building combines traditional and modern in its architecture and decorative elements, and is filled with reminders of Robin's life and personality, most charmingly in the oak carvings of animals and birds, inspired by his deep love of the natural world.

Address Thistle Foundation, Niddrie Mains Road, EH16 4EA, +44 (0)131 661 3366, www.robinchapel.org.uk | **Getting there** Lothian Buses 2, 14 or 30 to Niddrie Mains Road (Thistle Foundation) | **Hours** Sun 4pm–5pm, sung evensong, open to all | **Tip** Craigsbank Parish Church, in the west of the city, is another hidden gem of post-war architecture. Built in 1966, it has an innovative arena-style design, inspired by the hillside hollows where the 17th-century Covenanters preached (Craigs Bank, Corstorphine, EH12 8HD).

86 Rosslyn Chapel

A unique medieval puzzle

There is, quite simply, nowhere in the world like Rosslyn Chapel. From medieval times onwards, writers have struggled to define its stylistic features and describe its peculiar fascination. Its curious symbolism and iconography have made it the subject of a lot of fanciful speculation, since way before the fatuous hokum of *The Da Vinci Code* brought it worldwide fame: the earliest discovery of America and the true nature of the Stone of Destiny are just two of many mysteries it has been linked with.

The reason for all this is the chapel's extraordinary interior decoration. Entering the building is like walking into a three-dimensional puzzle; the mass of intricate stone carving that encrusts every available surface is initially quite overwhelming. It's only with time and effort that you can begin to make out some of the detail – among the burgeoning foliage, flowers and stars are angels, devils, saints, sinners, animals, birds and mythical beasts, all playing their parts in the sculptural extravaganza. There are over 100 depictions of the leafy pagan spirit known as the Green Man, though you're unlikely to spot more than a couple. Much easier to see is the *tour-de-force* Apprentice Pillar, said to represent the Nordic Tree of Life, with dragons nibbling at its roots, but also, in its spiralling structure, referring to the biblical Temple of Solomon. An old tale claims that this column was the initiative of a trainee mason, later murdered by his jealous master for demonstrating his own superior skill.

All this profligate ornamentation was highly unusual in the austere context of medieval Scottish architecture, and 'artificers from foreign kingdoms' had to be summoned by its founder, William Sinclair, when work began in the 1450s. Intriguingly, the chapel is only a fraction of the vast church he intended to build: now, that really would have been something else!

Address Chapel Loan, Roslin, Midlothian, EH25 9PU, +44 (0)131 440 2159, www.rosslynchapel.com | Getting there Lothian Buses 37 to Roslin (Original Rosslyn Hotel); journey time 45–60 mins from Edinburgh city centre | Hours Mon–Sat 9am–5pm, Sun noon–5pm; online booking advisable | Tip A brief stroll down the lane behind the chapel takes you to the partially ruined Rosslyn Castle, above the ruggedly scenic wooded gorge of Roslin Glen. The Castle is available as a holiday let; see www.landmarktrust.org.uk for details.

87 Sam Burns' Yard

From a needle to an anchor

The days are long gone when rag and bone men plied the Edinburgh streets, scrap merchants advertised their trade in horseshoes and rabbit skins, and a home could be kitted out with second-hand goods for a couple of pounds. But, amazingly, something of this lost world still survives in a rambling yard on the coast road just east of the city.

In 1947, Samuel Burns from Prestonpans set up in business as a firewood merchant on the site of a former quarry, behind the walls of the Prestongrange estate. He travelled the Lothians collecting old furniture from house sales, to chop up and sell as kindling for the coal fires that then heated everyone's homes. But passers-by often spotted a wardrobe or table that they wanted to buy, and Sam realised that the second-hand trade would be more lucrative. Soon the whole yard was full of anything that might sell, 'from a needle to an anchor', as his motto declared. Some of the goods were piled up in makeshift shelters, but turnover was so high that much of his stock was kept out in the open, in all weathers. The yard's fame grew, attracting couples setting up home, collectors in search of a bargain, and artists looking for interesting finds to include in their work.

This remarkable emporium by the sea is now run by Sam's grandsons, but little else seems to have changed in the past half-century. Even the phone in the enquiries cabin sounds with the nostalgic double ring of a black Bakelite receiver. A leisurely wander around the yard, down jumbled lanes of toilets and washbasins, through stacks of books, magazines, doors and windows, past once-treasured golf clubs, children's scooters and favourite armchairs, is a surreal experience. It's a journey into past lives that often feels like a tour of an impromptu art installation. You might not find a needle or an anchor at first, but you can always keep looking.

Address Woodend, Prestongrange, Prestonpans, EH32 9SA, +44 (0)1875 810 600, www.facebook.com/samburns.yard | Getting there Lothian Buses 26 to Prestongrange (Burns Yard) | Hours Mon–Sat 9.30am–4pm, Sun 11am–4pm | Tip For a complete change of scene, take the 26 bus (destination Seton Sands), a couple of miles east along the coast, and alight at West Lorimer Place to visit Cockenzie House and Garden. The 17th-century manor house is now a community arts venue with regular exhibitions and events, and a café (22 Edinburgh Road, daily 10am–5pm).

88 Sandy Bell's

The soul of Scots music

Folk music is the heartbeat of Scottish culture, and you can hear it every night at Sandy Bell's, played not for money but for pure pleasure. Sessions vary according to the day – Mondays are usually the province of fiddlers, followed by exponents of the 'moothie' (harmonica); on Wednesdays there are normally vocalists, and on alternate Thursdays younger singer-songwriters have their turn. But nothing is predictable. Traditional melodies and reels, often played in the distinctive style known as 'Edinburgh swing', can break out spontaneously at any time, as the energy and rhythms rise and draw more players into the session. And of course it depends on who's in town, because Sandy Bell's has for decades been a magnet for folk musicians from around the world.

Its origins as a music venue go back to 1942, but it was in the early 1950s that the pub became the favoured 'howff' of Hamish Henderson, a lecturer at the university's School of Scottish Studies, and a key figure in the Scottish folk revival. During the 1960s virtually everyone who was anyone on the folk scene played or sang in the bar's back room, and many honed their skills there – names like Barbara Dickson, Johnny and Phil Cunningham, Dick Gaughan, Dougie Maclean, Rab Noakes and Gerry Rafferty still resonate – and it was Arthur Argo, a regular stalwart, who persuaded the brilliant Shetland fiddler Aly Bain to quit his job as a joiner and move to the mainland to play professionally.

Music continues to rule at Sandy Bell's – though the range of beers and whiskies is very good too, and nowadays you can even get food. In years long gone, licensees tried to install attractions like jukeboxes, fruit machines and TV sets, but the regulars simply pitched them out on to the pavement. As the late manager Jimmy Cairney used to say, 'This place is full of revolutionaries who want nothing to change'.

Address 25 Forrest Road, EH1 2QH, +44 (0)131 225 2751, www.sandybells.com | Getting there Lothian Buses 2, 9, 23, 27, 35 or 45 to Forrest Road | Hours Mon–Sat noon–1am, Sun 12.30pm–midnight | Tip Five minutes' walk away at 14–16 Grassmarket are the stylish, purpose-built studios of Dance Base. Its year-round programme includes classes, workshops and events for all ages, levels and abilities in an exceptionally wide range of dance activity (www.dancebase.co.uk).

89_ Sciennes Jewish Burial Ground

A hidden cemetery for a hidden people

The district of Sciennes, just south-west of the Meadows, owes its name (pronounced 'sheens') to the short-lived 16th-century convent of Saint Catherine of Siena, founded by a group of widows after the Battle of Flodden, but disbanded during the Reformation. The convent fell into ruins, but nearly three centuries later, a congregation of a different religious faith chose a pocket of land near its remains as their final resting place.

Though not established until 1820, the Sciennes cemetery was the first, and for some years, the only Jewish burial ground in Scotland, serving communities throughout the country. The earliest synagogue in Edinburgh had been founded only four years earlier, in an apartment off nearby Nicolson Street. Like the Jewish community itself, the graveyard was small and unobtrusive, originally tucked away down a lane behind Sciennes Hill House – now gone, but once famed as the site of the only meeting between Robert Burns and the young Walter Scott.

Few people passing this cemetery today notice anything unusual about it. The graves look little different from Christian ones, with similarly shaped headstones arranged in lines or standing against the old enclosing walls. But a longer inspection reveals unfamiliar inscriptions, Jewish insignia and Hebraic characters. Four generations of some families were interred here before the ground was closed to burials in 1870. Many of the gravestones are now, poignantly, quite indecipherable. One is so weathered that the letters have been turned into wind-ruffled ripples; on another the elements have worn a hole right through the soft sandstone, leaving an empty space where the name should be. At the centre of Jewish worship is the Holy of Holies; behind its curtain there is nothing, for Jehovah cannot be seen. The deceased lying in this tomb has now truly vanished into eternity.

Address Sciennes House Place, EH9 1NW | Getting there Lothian Buses 12 to Causewayside (Sciennes House Place) | Hours Viewable from outside only | Tip A few minutes' walk away on the edge of the Meadows, the long-established Victor Hugo Continental Delicatessen is a good place for coffee, lunch or a snack (26/27 Melville Terrace; www.victorhugodeli.com).

90_Scotland Street Station

The railway under the New Town

The recent return of trams to Edinburgh's streets after 58 years (late, over-budget and under-used – but that's another story) has sparked interest in reviving other parts of its once extensive public transport network. No one, however, has so far called for the reopening of the underground rail tunnel in the heart of the city, and in fact few people are aware that such a thing exists. More surprising still is its location, beneath the polite streets known vicariously to a worldwide public through Alexander McCall Smith's *44 Scotland Street* novels. The great writer Robert Louis Stevenson described his boyhood fascination with this tunnel, and the thrill of watching trains 'shooting out of its dark maw' into Scotland Street Station. Originally part of the Edinburgh, Leith and Granton Railway, the long-abandoned station's site is now occupied by a park and children's playground.

In the 1840s, the company decided to extend the line south from Scotland Street to a terminus in the city centre, at what is now Waverley. This involved cutting a passage almost 1,000 metres long through solid rock, under residential streets, at a depth of up to 15 metres and on a steep gradient that reaches 1 in 27. But in 1862 the tunnel was abandoned, after only 15 years of operation. It was later used as a mushroom farm, an air-raid shelter, an experimental laboratory and a garage.

Long since unused, it's sealed off behind a firmly gated portal, and subterranean explorers these days have to content themselves with the shallower, 164-metre Rodney Street tunnel, on the opposite side of the park. Now a cycle path, it's light and airy enough to be a pleasant shortcut for pedestrians, and it has also been a venue for art projects. Sadly, no schemes are as yet forthcoming for the renovation of its companion, which must be a contender for the title of the world's longest short-lived tunnel.

Address King George V & Scotland Yard Parks, Eyre Place, EH3 5EN. Rodney Street Tunnel is part of National Cycle Route 75; the entrance to Scotland Street Tunnel is in the southeast corner. | Getting there Lothian Buses 8, 23, 27 or 36 to Canonmills, then walk down Canon Street and Logan Street to the park entrance | Tip The southern end of the Scotland Street tunnel can be seen at Waverley Station on Princes Street, identified by a prominent sign above a gated entrance in a wall opposite Platform 19.

91 The Scott Monument

One man and his dog

The soaring Gothic shrine that towers over the east end of Princes Street is such a familiar part of Edinburgh's streetscape that few passers-by give it a second glance, or pause to admire the marble statue seated under its massive open arches. For a 19th-century author of international renown, Sir Walter Scott cuts a surprisingly modest figure, sympathetically portrayed by sculptor John Steell with a large, elegant hound at his side.

Scott was famously fond of dogs, and always had one walking at his heels. He cancelled a dinner engagement in his grief on the death of his favourite bull terrier, Camp. Dandie Dinmont, a character from one of his novels, gave his name to a type of terrier, and Scott was himself an amateur breeder. When he went visiting he often took his hosts the gift of a puppy, generally called Pepper, Ginger, or Mustard, according to its colour. (Not all of the recipients' reactions are known, though the poet Wordsworth and his family became very fond of their Pepper.) But Scott's dearest canine companion, immortalised in marble beside him, was his deerhound Maida, named after a battle in the Napoleonic Wars. Maida predeceased the author by eight years, and has his own sculpted tomb at Scott's home, Abbotsford.

Completed in 1844, the Scott Monument is the largest memorial to a writer in the world. The competition for its design was won by George Meikle Kemp, a self-taught architect of humble origins who had made detailed studies of Gothic abbeys and cathedrals in Scotland and France, and assumed the alias of medieval mason John Morvo for his entry. Sadly, he accidentally drowned in the Union Canal shortly before the project was completed.

Though they're hard to make out on the soot-blackened exterior, the monument includes 68 statues of characters from Scott's novels, plus two more dogs, and a solitary pig.

Address East Princes Street Gardens, EH2 2EJ, +44 (0)131 529 4068 | Getting there Lothian Buses 3, 25, 26, 31 or 33 to Princes Street (Scott Monument) | Hours Interior: daily, Apr–Sept 10am–12.30pm & 1.45–4.30pm, Oct–Mar 10am–12.30pm & 1.45–3.30pm | Tip On the path by the monument's south-east corner is a bench dedicated to an international celebrity of a very different era, John Lennon. Lennon was a regular visitor to the city as a youngster, staying with relatives at 15 Ormidale Terrace, a house he enquired about buying shortly before he was killed.

92 The Sheep Heid Inn

Beer and skittles fit for a king

Unlike other historic villages now swallowed up by Edinburgh's suburbia, the attractive little community of Duddingston has never lost its character, and it still has a pub with an authentic village ambience. It's only a 25-minute bus ride from the centre, but if you decide to walk there instead through Holyrood Park, skirting the great hill of Arthur's Seat, or perhaps taking the path over the top, you'll certainly feel you've earned some liquid refreshment when you reach your destination.

The inn known as the Sheep Heid (pronounced 'heed' – meaning head) claims to have origins dating back to 1360, which would make it Scotland's oldest existing pub. This remains unproven, but it certainly has a very long and distinguished history. Situated halfway between the royal residences of Craigmillar Castle and the Palace of Holyroodhouse, it was a convenient resting place *en route* for the court. James VI is known to have stopped here regularly for sustenance, and the pub's name supposedly derives from a ram's head snuffbox, which he presented as a token of his gratitude. A replica of this relic is on display – though it seems an odd choice of gift from a man who wrote a fierce diatribe against tobacco, and it's more likely that the name originates from Duddingston's former culinary speciality. The village was for centuries the place of slaughter for the sheep that grazed in Holyrood Park, and resourceful locals used the heads, which were unsaleable, to make dishes like broth and roasts. These became so famous that they got a special footnote in Mrs Beeton's classic 1861 cookbook.

Sheep's heids no longer feature on the pub's menu, but another, more palatable attraction is still going strong. The traditional skittles alley is the oldest in Scotland; it dates from 1880, and is said to be on the site of a much earlier one where the king himself enjoyed knocking down the ninepins.

Address 43–45 The Causeway, Duddingston, EH15 3QA, +44 (0)131 661 7974, www.thesheepheidedinburgh.co.uk | Getting there Lothian Buses 12 to Duddingston Road West (Village); for walking routes, see www.historicenvironment.scot for the official map of Holyrood Park | Hours Mon–Sat noon–11pm, Sun noon–10.30pm. Advance booking essential for skittles alley. | Tip Two centuries-old curiosities can be seen just outside the gates to the nearby kirk: the iron punishment collar known as jougs, and the loupin' on stane, a stepped platform to help female or elderly parishioners – and, conceivably, the inn's inebriated customers – to get on horseback without loss of dignity.

93__Springvalley Gardens Lane

Ghost town in Morningside

In Glasgow, with its well-known affection for American popular culture, a back alley of workshops converted into what looks like a Western film set would raise few eyebrows. But Edinburgh is not a city where anyone would imagine finding such a place, and the fact that this alley is located just behind the main street in the legendarily genteel district of Morningside is an even bigger surprise.

This lovingly detailed recreation of a Wild West township was built in the mid-1990s by Michael Faulkner, son of the last prime minister of Northern Ireland, and owner at that time of the Great American Indoors, a company trading in Santa Fe-style furniture of his own design. As a promotion for his store he employed artists, including two fresh from Euro Disney in France, to create 'the full John Ford'. The lane was soon transformed into the enclave they knew as El Pedro, with clapboard and adobe frontages announcing the entrances to a saloon, cantina, jailhouse, livery station and sheriff's office.

It was all a façade of course, and an expensive, if delightful, indulgence. In 2001 Faulkner's furniture business went bust, and the lane, formerly populated by ceramicists and other craftspeople, soon reverted to the more usual domain of garages and mechanics' workshops. The whole scene now has a suitably ghost-town look, weathered not by the searing New Mexico sun, but the blustery Scottish rain. A discreet notice on the cantina's entrance tells you to keep clear, for it is in fact the fire exit for Morningside Library.

In a strange way, the make-believe in this alley is less out of place than it might seem. When the American West was being colonised, Morningside was little more than a row of simple cottages on the edge of the city, a frontier settlement not all that different from El Paso.

Address Springvalley Gardens, EH10 4QF | Getting there Lothian Buses 5, 11, 15, 16, 23 or 36 to Morningside Road (Springvalley Gardens) | Tip A few minutes' walk south, there is a grim reminder of the rough justice meted out to outlaws in the Edinburgh of two centuries ago. The Hanging Stanes, in the roadway outside 66 Braid Road, mark the place where in 1815 a gallows was specially erected, on the site of a robbery, for the execution of two highwaymen.

94 St Bernard's Well

The foul waters of Hygeia

The woodland path through the valley of the Water of Leith is today one of the most delightful places in the city for a peaceful stroll, but it wasn't always so pleasant. In the late 18th century the fast flowing river became so polluted with sewage that it was crudely nicknamed 'Tumble Turd'. It was, nonetheless, a very fashionable place for 'taking the waters' – not of the river, but from a mineral spring, in the pump room beneath the temple of St Bernard's Well.

The spring was supposedly discovered in 1760 by three schoolboys who were fishing on the riverbank; its name derives from a legend that the 12th-century St Bernard of Clairvaux lived in a nearby cave. Though the flavour of the water was once likened to 'the washings of a foul gunbarrel', it was widely valued as a digestive tonic, and was believed to cure a variety of complaints including joint pain, impotence, and 'all the diseases of a lax and weak fibre'. Customers paid good money – 5 shillings – for a season's subscription to the well, and they were often there at dawn, as the water was claimed to be most effective between 6am and 9am.

Commissioned in 1789 by appreciative imbiber Lord Gardenstone, the wellhead was designed by Alexander Nasmyth, a celebrated landscape painter. Nasmyth had studied in Italy, and he created a perfect little classical enclave beneath the trees, inspired by the Temple of Vesta at Tivoli, near Rome. A statue of the goddess Hygeia stands among the Doric columns of the rotunda, guarding the pump room below. In 1887 the then owner, William Nelson, had its interior redecorated with a stunning golden sunburst mosaic, and a marble pedestal for the pump inscribed *Bibendo valebis* ('By drinking you will become well'). Nelson later gifted the well to the city of Edinburgh, for the benefit of all; however, the council long ago declared its pungent water unsafe to drink.

Address Water of Leith walkway, between Deanhaugh Street and Dean Bridge, EH4 | Getting there Lothian Buses 24 or 29 to Kerr Street; join the path by the bridge at Saunders Street and walk upriver | Hours Normally viewable from the outside only; access to pump room interior on occasional Sundays in summer | Tip Stockbridge Market is held every Sunday at Jubilee Gardens, by the bridge. A wide range of fresh produce is available, as well as a variety of street food, craft items and clothing (Sun 10am–5pm).

95 St Cecilia's Hall

Listening to the 18th century

The patron saint of music, from whom St Cecilia's Hall takes its name, was according to legend an Early Christian martyr, put to death by suffocation and a clumsy attempted beheading. In the 1960s this fine 18th-century building had ignominies visited on it that, in architectural terms, were every bit as brutal and inept, and left its entrance, on a cramped street off the insalubrious Cowgate, looking grimly like a public toilet.

As a result, this little gem, one of the Old Town's finest historic halls, was for many decades an extremely well-hidden treasure. All that however is thankfully in the past, as the complex has now been sympathetically restored to its original character, and has even had its former acoustic recreated.

Completed in 1763, St Cecilia's is Scotland's oldest purpose-built concert hall. It's said to be the only place in the world today where you can regularly listen to 18th-century music played on original instruments in a purpose-built room of the same period – a lovely domed, elliptical space. The Edinburgh Musical Society, an association of amateur musicians founded in 1728, commissioned it as a venue for their concerts by professional musicians and singers. These often came from far afield, such as the Italian castrato Tenducci – notoriously married – who enchanted audiences there in May 1769 with his performance in the opera *Artaxerxes*.

The new St Cecilia's complex incorporates a large gallery space showcasing Edinburgh University's internationally important collection of historic musical instruments, which includes more than 4,000 items. Of particular significance and beauty are the early keyboard instruments, dating from the 16th century onwards, most of which are maintained in playing condition. These include harpsichords with delicate marquetry and exquisitely painted lids, and curiosities such as the euphonicon, or harp piano.

Address Niddry Street, EH1 1NQ, www.stcecilias.ed.ac.uk | Getting there Lothian Buses 5, 7, 8, 14, 35, 45 or 49 to South Bridge, or 35 to High Street | Hours Tue–Sat 10am–5pm; see website for programme of talks, guided tours and workshops, plus evening concerts | Tip Just round the corner is the Museum of Childhood, the first in the world to specialise in the subject, with displays that appeal to nostalgic adults as well as children (42 High Street, EH1 1TG, daily 10am–5pm).

96 St Margaret's Chapel

Simple shrine for a sainted queen

On the topmost outcrop of Castle Rock stands a humble ancient chapel, whose very survival is remarkable in view of the turbulent history it has witnessed. Dating from the early 12th century, the shrine dedicated to St Margaret is the oldest surviving structure within the complex of Edinburgh Castle, and indeed the oldest building by far in the whole city. Today it remains as it was always intended to be: a simple little oasis of peace, set apart from the great bastion of war.

Margaret was a Saxon princess, born in exile in Hungary, and forced to flee England after the Norman invasion of 1066. When the ship carrying her to the continent was blown off course, she landed instead in southern Scotland, and was taken to Edinburgh. There she met the king, Malcolm Canmore – son of Duncan, and successor to Macbeth – and became his queen. A strong, well-educated and devout woman, famed for her charitable work, she soon set about civilising her rough-and-ready adoptive country, and became a prime mover in the reform of the Scottish church. It was Margaret who encouraged the king to move the capital south from Dunfermline and establish a royal residence on Edinburgh's Castle Rock. She died in her chamber there in 1093, shortly after hearing of her husband's death in battle.

Although Margaret wasn't officially canonised until 1249, it's thought that her pious son King David I established the chapel on the rock in her memory within a few decades of her death. The building fell into decline during the Reformation, and was later used as a storehouse for gunpowder, but restoration began soon after it was rediscovered in 1845. The sensitive stained glass was added in the 20th century, but otherwise the chapel is now much as it was when it was built, around nine centuries ago. It was reconsecrated in 1934, and baptisms, weddings and other services are still held there.

Address Edinburgh Castle, Castlehill, EH1 2NG, +44 (0)131 225 9846, www.edinburghcastle.scot; the Chapel is in the Upper Ward, through Foog's Gate | Getting there Lothian Buses 9, 23 or 27 to George IV Bridge | Hours Daily: Apr–Sept 9.30am–6pm; Oct–Mar 9.30am–5pm (last entry 1 hour earlier) | Tip The Honours of Scotland, the oldest set of royal regalia in Britain, are on display in the Crown Room of the castle's Royal Palace. The crown, sword and sceptre were first used together in 1543, for the coronation of the infant Mary, Queen of Scots.

97_St Triduana's Chapel

Spiritual cleansing

According to legend, Triduana was a devout Christian maiden who lived in Scotland around the 6th century. The Pictish King Nectan fell in love with her, praising in particular the beauty of her eyes until, fed up with his pestering, she plucked them out and sent them to him, skewered on a thorn. Triduana then became famed for her skill in curing eye diseases, a proficiency that persisted after her death. On the site of her burial at Restalrig a natural spring arose; a shrine was built, and pilgrims afflicted with blindness and poor sight came from far and near to bathe their eyes in its holy healing waters.

The Gothic chapel, or well-house, that still bears Triduana's name is a remarkable hexagonal vault, half underground, next to the parish church of Restalrig, a quiet little enclave just a short way east of the city centre. The chapel, which originally had a grander upper storey, was built in the 1470s on the orders of King James III, and was described by Pope Innocent VIII as 'sumptuous'. By the mid-16th century Restalrig, now a Collegiate Church with a dean, singing boys and 32 altars, was one of the main centres of Roman Catholicism in Scotland, and as such it became an early focus for the vitriol of Protestant firebrand John Knox. He preached that all 'monuments to idolatry' were to be 'cast down', and in 1560 the religious buildings at Restalrig were duly razed to the ground – though not quite.

In 1906 the lower chamber of St Triduana's Chapel, complete with its central pier and ribbed vaulting, was discovered under a grassy knoll. It had somehow survived Knox's spiritual cleansing, perhaps because it was used, for a while, as a burial vault for the local lairds. But it could be that pious locals had concealed it, to preserve its healing powers. Until recently, believers continued to come and cleanse their eyes in the water that still wells up from under the floor.

Address St Margaret's Parish Church, 176 Restalrig Road South, EH7 6EA, +44 (0)131 554 7400 | Getting there Lothian Buses 19 or 34 to Marionville Road (Restalrig) | Hours Contact church (now known as LARCH Restalrig) to arrange a visit, by phone or email: mail@larch.co.uk | Tip Set into the slope beside Queen's Drive, just south-east of Holyrood Palace, is St Margaret's Well, an atmospheric miniature version of St Triduana's Chapel. It was moved to its present site from Restalrig in 1860.

98 The Stockbridge Colonies

By the workers, for the workers

A stranger in town might be surprised to hear Edinburgh locals talking blithely about houses in the colonies; most would assume that they were referring to spacious bungalows in some far-flung part of the former British Empire. But Edinburgh's colony houses are far removed from the verandahs of expat tea planters, retired colonels and gin-swilling memsahibs; they were the product of a pioneering 19th-century scheme to provide decent, well-built and affordable homes for skilled working men and their families.

These model dwellings were constructed by the Edinburgh Co-operative Building Company, founded in 1861 as a direct result of a strike by construction workers, who were demanding a reduction in their 10-hour working day. Most employers responded by refusing to allow them back on site, and many men lost their jobs as a result. But a small group of stonemasons then reacted by taking the brave initiative of forming their own limited liability construction company, which soon attracted dozens of shareholders from every building trade, as well as the support of prominent churchmen and other influential citizens who were concerned with improving the living conditions of the workers.

The company bought a parcel of land in the district of Stockbridge, then a semi-rural area, and in October 1861 the foundation stone was laid for their first scheme of 11 parallel terraces of 'flatted cottages'. The ingenious double-faced design allowed each family house to have a private entrance, and its own front garden. An outside staircase led to an apartment on the upper two floors, while the door to the ground floor flat was on the other side of the building.

The homes were an immediate success, and over the following 15 years another 10 sites, mainly on the fringes of the city, were similarly 'colonised'. Unsurprisingly, the attractive development at Stockbridge has since become gentrified.

Address The 11 terraces of the Colonies start at Reid Terrace, EH3 5JH | Getting there Lothian Buses 24 or 29 to Raeburn Place, then walk down St Bernard's Row and cross the bridge; the terraces run between Glenogle Road and the Water of Leith | Tip Two other groups of colony flats near the city centre are the terraces off Dalry Place, near Haymarket, and those at Abbeyhill, off London Road at East Norton Place.

99_Summerhall

Artful revamp of the old vet school

When Robert McDowell bought Edinburgh University's former Veterinary School building in 2011, it was with the declared aim of creating an arts complex unlike any other. Adopting the name of its Southside location, Summerhall opened its doors for the Fringe Festival in August of that year, and was immediately lauded by press and public alike as an exceptional new venue. It soon grew to become Europe's biggest private arts centre, an unconventional vortex of year-round creative activity where virtually any form of artistic expression might be encountered, from cutting-edge theatre, exhibitions and music to kids' shows and ceilidhs.

Like his brainchild, McDowell is eccentric, eclectic, and resolutely unbureaucratic. An economist with a former career in journalism, he is also a trained artist who worked for 20 years with Edinburgh impresario Richard Demarco, and was once an assistant to Joseph Beuys. For decades McDowell had been formulating his ideas for an arts centre when the building came on the market, and a substantial family legacy enabled him to realise his dream.

The vast complex – once familiarly known, after the school's founder, as the Dick Vet – is an amorphous, labyrinthine hotchpotch of labs, dissection rooms, offices and lecture halls, and this lends a unique quality to Summerhall's performance spaces and galleries. Many of the rooms retain fittings like fume cupboards, operating tables and gas taps, and the Anatomy Lecture Theatre still has its traditional curved benches. The Small Animal Hospital is now occupied by the quirkily furnished Royal Dick pub, where you can sample the products of the in-house brewery. There are also around 120 artists and creative businesses based within the cultural village. There was widespread dismay in 2024 at the announcement of a financial crisis that threatened the future of the venue, but this was thankfully averted, and Summerhall's unique cultural mission continues.

Address 1 Summerhall Place, EH9 1PL, +44 (0)131 560 1580, www.summerhall.co.uk | Getting there Lothian Buses 12 to Summerhall, or 2, 3, 5, 7, 8, 29, 30, 31, 33, 37, 47, 47B or 49 to South Clerk Street | Hours Open daily from 9am; see website for events programme | Tip Five minutes' walk away at 85–89 Clerk Street, EH8 9JG, the Queen's Hall is a more conventional arts venue housed in a converted church, with a year-round programme mainly of high-quality classical, jazz and folk music (www.thequeenshall.net).

100 Surgeons' Hall Museums

Gruesome, but gripping

Though its grand neoclassical façade may make Surgeons' Hall appear exclusive, you certainly don't have to be a medical professional to enter its august portals today, and within the enclave you'll find a museum that should be of genuine interest to everyone. Most people know very little about the inside of their own bodies, and still less about what actually happens when they go – as many of us have done, or will do at some point – under the surgeon's knife. But be warned – the evidence of all sorts of diseases and deformities is laid bare in the displays, and some of the exhibits are definitely not for the squeamish.

The museum, which houses collections first instituted in 1699, has recently reopened after a major refurbishment. Previously rather an unsettling place, full of dark corners and macabre surprises, it's now an airy galleried space devoted to education and enlightenment. The new display allows visitors to view thousands of pathology specimens and surgical tools, as well as a great many less clinical exhibits. Though the aim is far from sensational, there is still the occasional, compellingly gruesome item, such as a pocket book covered with the skin of the notorious William Burke, who together with his accomplice William Hare murdered 16 people, whose bodies were then sold to the ill-famed Dr Robert Knox for dissection.

One highlight of the new display is the mock-up of an 18th-century anatomy theatre, complete with 'digital cadaver', where visitors can experience a fascinating recreation of Scotland's first public dissection, as carried out by Archibald Pitcairn over the course of a week in 1702. There is also a space devoted to Joseph Bell, the teacher of Arthur Conan Doyle, which includes a remarkable film in which the author (speaking with a distinctive Scottish burr) gives full credit to the doctor with astonishing deductive powers who was the inspiration for Sherlock Holmes.

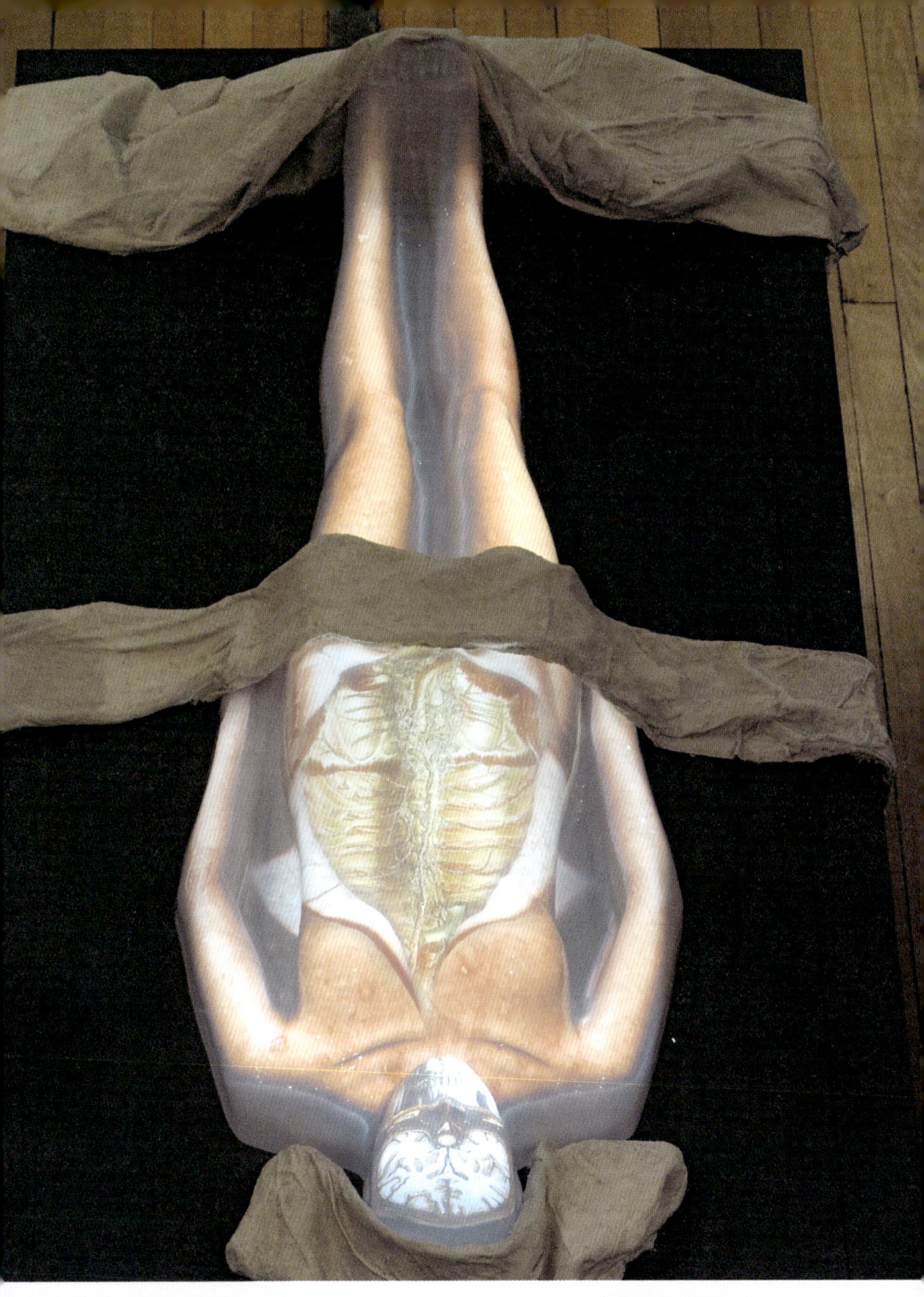

Address Royal College of Surgeons of Edinburgh, Nicolson Street, EH8 9DW, +44 (0) 0131 527 1600, www.museum.rcsed.ac.uk | Getting there Lothian Buses 2, 3, 5, 8, 14, 30, 33 or 49 to Nicolson Street (Hill Place) | Hours Daily 10am–5pm | Tip Five minutes' walk south on the main road, Kalpna is an inventive Indian vegetarian restaurant, long renowned for its all-you-can-eat lunchtime buffet (2–3 St Patrick Square, daily noon–2.30pm & 5.30–10.30pm).

101_Swanston

A quaint little place in the lap of the hills

Scotland is a country in which chocolate-box villages are rather thin on the ground, and a charming hamlet like Swanston is an extreme rarity. Despite its name, there's no pond here with waterfowl, but it has all the other classic picturesque ingredients, with its group of whitewashed thatched cottages set in rolling lawns, sheltered by woodland and flanking a gurgling brook. The village is just beyond the southern suburbs of Edinburgh, on the lower slopes of the Pentland Hills, below a golf course. There's no through road – visitors have to leave their cars in the parking area outside, or walk a good way from the nearest bus stop. Only the continuous drone of distant traffic on the city bypass mars the tranquillity of what is otherwise an idyllic rural oasis.

The village, at the foot of the Pentland Hills, started life as Sveins Tun, the old Norse name for a farm that was recorded on the site in 1214. The Swanston of today had its origins in 1761, when Edinburgh town council established a waterworks here to boost the city's supply, and in addition built a cottage, which was later enlarged into a rambling two-storey house. This was to become a favourite haunt of Robert Louis Stevenson, whose father rented it as a summer home for his family between 1867 and 1880. The young writer grew very fond of the house, its surroundings, and the local people, particularly the shepherd John Todd, 'all his days faithful to that curlew-scattering, sheep-collecting life'. Memories of the place remained with him on his travels up until the end of his short life, last surfacing in his novel *St Ives*, left unfinished on his untimely death.

Swanston had no electricity supply until 1949, and the old cottages, originally built for shepherds and other farmworkers, were semi-derelict when in 1964 Edinburgh council had them sympathetically restored, and rethatched with reeds from the River Tay.

Address Swanston Village, EH10 7DT | **Getting there** Lothian Buses 4 or 400 to Oxgangs Road (Swanston Road), then a half-mile walk due south | **Tip** Continue your walk up into the Pentland Hills Regional Park. A noticeboard in the car park just below the village gives information on various signposted routes, and on the history and natural features of the area.

102 Thomson's Tower

The curling club and the painting minister

The sport of curling is essentially a form of bowls, played on ice with flat-bottomed granite stones. It originated in Scotland in medieval times, but it was at the beginning of the 19th century that the rules of the game were first formulated, by the Duddingston Curling Society. This was a prestigious Edinburgh club, formed by peers, advocates, landowners, academics and the like, who had been forced to find a new venue for their favourite winter sport after the construction of the New Town began, and their previous haunt, the Nor' Loch, was drained. After trying out various ponds and other stretches of water around the city, they finally settled on Duddingston Loch, where the society was founded in 1795.

They erected a small building at the water's edge to store their stones and curling brooms – used to sweep the ice in front of speeding stones and influence their trajectory. This proved inadequate as the society grew, and in 1825 the architect William Henry Playfair took time out from building neoclassical temples to design a delightful little octagonal tower for the members. The curling equipment was kept on the lower floor, while the upper storey was used for socialising after games. Conviviality was an important part of the sport.

The season for curling was of course limited, and this suited the minister of nearby Duddingston Kirk, the Reverend John Thomson, a keen amateur painter, who was able to use the upper room as his studio during the many months when play was impossible. Thomson's dramatic coastal landscapes earned him a well-deserved reputation, and he was acquainted with many celebrated professional artists, including J. M. W. Turner, who admired the outlook from his unusual studio. The tower later fell into dereliction, but in the late 20th century the land it occupies became part of what is now Dr Neil's Garden (see ch. 28), and it was thanks to the garden's trustees that it was finally restored in 2009. Further work was carried out in 2023.

Address Dr Neil's Garden, Old Church Lane, EH15 3PX, www.neilsgarden.co.uk | Getting there Lothian Buses 12 to Duddingston village. Dr Neil's Garden is through the gates to Duddingston Manse and along the path to the right; the Tower is by the lochside in the south-east corner of the garden | Hours Exterior: daily 10am–dusk; interior open on various dates in summer months for art exhibitions. It can also be hired for events; see website | Tip The National Galleries of Scotland have a number of fine paintings by the Rev. Thomson in their collection, as well as calotype portraits of him by photography pioneers Hill and Adamson.

103_The Treasure Trove

Homemade, fairtrade, self-aid

With the heyday of the department store long gone, and the ease of online ordering an inescapable reality, the glory days of the once proud shopping streets of central Edinburgh are now a distant memory. So it's all the more surprising to discover one modest little survivor, with values very different from the retail giants that were its former neighbours, still quietly trading on a prime site in the much-altered environment.

Its expertly handcrafted knitwear, baby clothes and soft toys, small gifts and accessories, home-made cakes and preserves make it a magnet for a small band of discerning locals – though most consumers, sweeping past in pursuit of their next fix of predictable retail therapy, don't even register its existence.

The Treasure Trove is the not-for-profit sales outlet of a unique survival, the Royal Edinburgh Repository and Self-Aid Society, constituted in 1977 as a consequence of the amalgamation of two charitable associations founded in the Victorian era. The aim of both was to help women in need, such as those forced to retire on insufficient means from posts in domestic service, and enable them to help themselves, by using their skills in needlework, knitting, baking, or other crafts. The original society began selling members' work in 1882, and the following year it opened its first shop, in the city's West End.

Membership is no longer restricted to 'indigent gentlewomen', and today's makers are people of all kinds with handicraft skills who clearly gain a reward that is more than merely financial out of what they do. The prices, set by the makers themselves, reflect this, and items such as hand-crocheted christening robes can often be found modestly placed at the back of a drawer. The shop will take orders for many sought-after items, ranging from Fair Isle waistcoats and Arran pullovers to hand-knitted Christmas nativity figures. Goods can also be viewed and ordered online, and posted out to you.

Address 23a Castle Street, EH2 3DN, +44 (0)131 220 1187, www.treasuretrove-edinburgh.com | Getting there Lothian Buses 1, 3, 4, 15, 19, 24, 26, 30, 31, 33, 34 or 44 to Princes Street West | Hours Mon–Sat 9am–5pm | Tip Around a mile away in the lively neighbourhood of Stockbridge, An Independent Zebra is another unique shop that's well worth seeking out. A champion of local makers and designers, it stocks a carefully curated selection of original homewear, furnishings, stationery and gifts (88–92 Raeburn Place).

104_Trinity Apse

A truncated Gothic relic

There is little evidence today of the glorious Gothic churches that graced the city in medieval times. Their mutilation began during the 16th-century Reformation, when mobs ripped out interior furnishings, and marauding troops, fires and modernising architects all later contributed to the loss of what remained. By the mid-19th century only one 15th-century church still stood largely unscathed, and the story of its ultimate fate is perhaps the saddest of all.

The construction of Trinity College Kirk began in 1460 on a site just south-west of Calton Hill. It was founded by Mary of Guelders in memory of her consort, King James II. Work continued until the 1530s, and though it was never completed as planned, the result was one of the finest churches in Scotland, a lofty structure with splendid flying buttresses and a soaring, vaulted interior.

In 1848 the North British Railway Company announced its plans to expand the sidings of Waverley Station into the area occupied by the church, which was then owned by the town council. Despite public protests, it was agreed that this could go ahead, on condition that the company paid for the building to be carefully dismantled and re-erected elsewhere. Each element was duly numbered, and the church was soon reduced to a sad heap of Gothic stonework, lying unprotected on Calton Hill. When a decision was finally reached on its new site in 1872, not only had a great many of the stones mysteriously vanished, but so had the funds for rebuilding, and only a partial reconstruction was possible.

Hidden down a little-used close and hemmed in by a grim 1960s' development, the building, whose grimy external walls still bear some painted numbers, is now reduced to a rump. Despite this, the interior is a grand, graceful space, but neither it nor the little side garden are normally open. No wonder the crumbling gargoyles seem to howl in dismay.

Address Chalmers Close, High Street, EH1 1SS | Getting there Lothian Buses 35 to Royal Mile (Chalmers Close) | Hours Normally viewable from outside only. It can also be seen from Trunk's Close, a few metres down the Royal Mile. | Tip The Trinity Panels by Hugo Van Der Goes, part of a monumental altarpiece commissioned for the church, are on display in the National Gallery of Scotland on the Mound (on loan from H.M. the King). Painted around 1475, these exceptional works of art are presumed to have escaped destruction by iconoclasts because they contain portraits of the royal family.

105 Trinity House

A better life on the ocean wave

Visitors to Leith who know it only from *Trainspotting* and other dystopian Irvine Welsh novels must surely be taken aback by the reality of the district today, with its social and cultural diversity, Michelin-starred restaurants, and tourist magnet of the Royal Yacht *Britannia*. But it isn't just these recent fruits of regeneration that make this much-maligned burgh worth discovering. Leith has a long history, and there are still some vivid reminders of its past glory as Scotland's chief port, among them the splendid neoclassical guild hall of Trinity House.

This was the headquarters of the ancient Incorporation of Masters and Mariners, which as long ago as 1380 was given the right to levy duty on merchant ships using the port. This income was used to help poor, sick and aged sailors and their families, and by 1555 the guild was prosperous enough to build an almshouse, whose cellars survive under the present early 19th-century building. Trinity House began offering formal nautical training in 1680, and it was soon issuing pilots' licences, and organising navigators for vessels entering Leith Docks. From an early date it helped to maintain coal-fired lights to guide shipping in the Firth of Forth, and it was later instrumental in planning and funding much more advanced lighthouses.

The Trinity House building, now in the care of Historic Scotland, still has its original furniture and fittings, including fine nautically themed ceiling decoration. A fascinating range of artefacts from its collections is on display, mostly laid out on a vast mahogany table in the magnificent convening room. There are many items relating to the mariners who manned the whaling fleets, some of which, like the quirky caricature Scotsman painted on a whale's ear, and the sensitive, bright-eyed penguin carved from a tooth, have a gentle charm that belies their harrowing origins.

Address 99 Kirkgate, Leith, EH6 6BJ, www.historicenvironment.scot/visit-a-place/places/trinity-house | **Getting there** Lothian Buses 7, 12, 14, 16, 21 or 35 to Great Junction Street (Kirkgate Centre) or Tram to Foot of the Walk. Trinity House is on the lane behind the shopping mall. | **Hours** Apr–Sept, Fri only, guided tours 1 & 3pm. Advance booking essential, via website | **Tip** The neo-Gothic South Leith Parish Church, just opposite, is well worth a visit; its fine interior includes a splendid hammerbeam roof, and it also has an intriguing graveyard.

106_ Tupiniquim Ex-Police Box

The afterlife of the bobbies' temples

The worldwide success of the BBC TV series *Dr Who*, whose hero travels through time and space in an outwardly normal police box, has turned a modest piece of street furniture into a global icon. When the show first aired in 1963, police boxes were a common sight in Britain's cities, and the Doctor's shape-shifting Tardis initially took that form so as to go unnoticed in a London backstreet.

The first police boxes appeared in the USA in the late 1870s, but most of these were no more than tiny booths housing emergency telephones. It was in 1920s' Britain that the concept grew into a kiosk large enough to contain a mini-police station, complete with desk, stool, lighting and heating. The wooden, square-plan 'Tardis' style of box soon sprouted across the UK – but Edinburgh had to be different. In 1931 the city architect of the Athens of the North, Ebenezer MacRae, came up with an appropriate original design. His roomier cast-iron structures were conceived as little Greek temples, rectangular in plan, with pediments, pilasters and classical wreaths, as well as window mouldings incorporating the saltire, or Scottish cross.

But mobile phones and changes in policing methods gradually rendered these noble boxes obsolete, and most of the 86 that used to grace the city's streets have now been sold off. Some have gone, but many of those remaining have been repainted – in any colour but police blue – and adapted for use as coffee kiosks and takeaway food stalls. One of the most enterprising is the popular Tupiniquim, whose Brazilian owners make what's arguably the tastiest and best value street food in the city – freshly cooked gluten-free crêpes with a choice of delicious fillings, and a wide range of freshly pressed juices, always served with a smile. It's healthy fare that's worth waiting for, and there's funky music, sometimes live, to entertain you as you queue.

Address Lauriston Place, on the corner of Middle Meadow Walk, EH1 9AU, www.tupiniquim.co.uk | **Getting there** Lothian Buses 12, 23, 27, 35, 45, 47 or 47B to Lauriston Place (Middle Meadow Walk) | **Hours** Mon–Sat noon–6pm; longer hours (including Sunday opening) in summer | **Tip** You'll find a variety of other ex-police box cafés dotted throughout the city. One long-established favourite with locals is the friendly Sam's Coffee Box, at the southwest corner of Bruntsfield Links. Apart from great coffee, it also serves baked goods and snacks (99a Bruntsfield Place).

107 Victoria Swing Bridge

Keeping the docks in full swing

The settlement of Leith originated in medieval times, around a haven with sheltered anchorage where Edinburgh's little river meets the Firth of Forth. Wharves were built there as early as the 12th century, and by the 16th century a prosperous waterfront town had grown up on both banks of the Water of Leith. A toll bridge upstream of the harbour, connecting lands owned by Holyrood Abbey, was for many years the only link between the two communities.

In the days when journeys were faster and easier by water, it was not only a cargo port but the primary point of entry into Scotland for passengers from the south, including royalty. But Leith was always mainly concerned with commerce, and the names of locations near the original harbour – Baltic Street, Cadiz Street and Timber Bush (a corruption of *bourse*, meaning exchange) – reveal evidence of its former trading links. The port grew vastly in the 19th century, as the quays were enlarged and new enclosed docks built, extending into the deeper waters of the Forth. It soon became essential to construct a connection across the water between the east and west sides of the port, capable of allowing shipping to pass, and in 1874 the hydraulically powered Victoria Swing Bridge was erected, an impressive wrought-iron structure carrying a roadway and double rail tracks. With its 37-metre clear span, the bridge was the largest of its kind in the UK.

By the mid-20th century the inner harbour had fallen into decline, and though it remained in use as a vehicle crossing until the 1990s, the bridge swung for the last time in 1964. In 2018, the ailing structure, long bereft of its road and railway, was added to the Buildings at Risk register, but happily it has since been fully refurbished for use by pedestrians and cyclists. Now guarding a transformed waterfront of residential and office developments, the emasculated swinger is still a powerful reminder of the port's heyday.

Address Ocean Drive, EH6 6QT | Getting there Lothian Buses 16, 34, 35 or 36 to The Shore, or Tram to Port of Leith | Tip The cylindrical building on the corner of Tower Street is one of the oldest buildings in Leith, dating from the 1680s. Originally a windmill, it was altered in 1805 to function as a signal tower, which let ships know the depth of the water at the harbour bar.

108 The Wee Museum of Memory

Remembrance of things past

The once prestigious shopping and leisure complex of Ocean Terminal has a poignant air about it today. Opened in 2001 on the site of a former shipyard, it was designed by the eminent Sir Terence Conran as the showplace of the revitalised Leith waterfront. But like so many retail centres across the UK, it has lately suffered a decline that has been described, inevitably, as terminal. The big name stores moved out long ago, and although it still serves as the entrance route to the tourist magnet of the Royal Yacht *Britannia*, part of it has been demolished and the remainder is now being 'reimagined'.

One happy beneficiary of this transitional period is the Living Memory Association, an enterprising community group who have found a fitting new home within the vacant units for their heritage and reminiscence centre, the Wee Museum of Memory. Founded in 1986, this inspired venture has since garnered a remarkable collection of more than 10,000 artefacts and photographs relating to everyday life in the city over the past 90 years or so, from antiquated typewriters, radios, and clocks that graced long-gone mantlepieces to vintage teapots, picnic sets and bathing costumes. What sets it apart from conventional museums of social history is that all of these items can be handled, an experience that stimulates sensations far more intense than those gained by peering at objects in a glass case. One of the most popular sections is packed with once-familiar kitchen utensils and fondly remembered comestibles like Creamola Foam, and there's an equally nostalgic children's area, filled with toys and games that are truly eye-opening for today's youngsters.

Visitors to the city are as welcome as locals, and the friendly staff hold regular reminiscence sessions where people of all backgrounds come together to share their personal stories of times gone by.

Address First floor, Ocean Terminal, Ocean Drive, EH54 6HR, +44 (0)7714 783726, www.livingmemory.org.uk | Getting there Lothian Buses 10, 34, 35, 36 or 200, or Tram to Ocean Terminal | Hours Mon–Fri 10.30am–4pm, Sat & Sun 11am–4pm | Tip Another valuable community project with a base at Ocean Terminal is the Leith Collective, whose spacious shop (also on the first floor) is filled with unique eco-friendly items made by local artists and crafters, all of them committed to sustainability and the reuse of materials.

109 The Wee Waddle

The zoo's perennial black-and-white stars

Edinburgh Zoo is a much-loved local institution, and there was huge excitement when in 2011 it took delivery of two giant pandas, on loan from China. They remained a massive draw until they were flown home in 2023, though the experience of crowding round a glass wall to watch these naturally solitary and unsociable animals was criticised by some as disturbingly voyeuristic, particularly in view of their failure to produce the anticipated cub. Fortunately, however, there are other charismatic black-and-white creatures still in residence who seem to positively enjoy public attention – the penguins.

The zoo has had a long association with these birds: its original six arrived from South Georgia in 1914, and in 1919 a king penguin chick was hatched here – the first in the world to be bred in captivity. The tradition of 'Penguin Parade' began by chance in 1951, when an adventurous gentoo wandered out of an unsecured gate. Intrigued, its keeper decided to let others follow, and led the troop around the zoo, to the delight of visitors. The supervised walks soon became a popular daily event.

The attraction was suspended for a time, due first to Covid and then the threat of bird flu, but it has now returned, reimagined as the Wee Waddle. This includes a feeding session as well as the chance for any penguins who wish to explore outside their habitat to enjoy a short excursion.

After the rush of exuberant gentoos and rockhoppers, the king penguins generally follow in a more stately fashion. At the end of the procession you'll often find Sir Nils Olaf III, mascot of the Norwegian Royal Guard, knighted in 2008 with the approval of a real king, Harald V. When the outing's over, they're happy to return to their enclosure – unsurprisingly, since it contains the largest penguin pool in the world. It's a joy to see these charming birds demonstrating their natural grace and agility in the water, after their delightful collective waddle.

Address Penguins Rock, Edinburgh Zoo, 134 Corstorphine Road, EH12 6TS | Getting there Lothian Buses 12, 26 or 31 to Corstorphine Road (Edinburgh Zoo) | Hours Zoo daily, Apr–Sept 10am–6pm, Mar & Oct 10am–5pm, Nov–Feb 10am–4pm; Wee Waddle autumn and winter only, Thu–Sun 2.15pm | Tip The zoo has an excellent programme of daily talks, plus a wide variety of tours, events and animal encounters for all ages; check website for details.

110 The Witches' Fountain

Fair is foul, and foul is fair

When Shakespeare constructed his 'Scottish play' around the three weird sisters, whose prophecies guide the dark deeds of Macbeth, he was reflecting the grim preoccupation of his own era with sorcery and dealings with the devil. This was an obsession of the reigning king, James I of England and VI of Scotland.

It was in 1563, in the reign of his mother Mary, Queen of Scots, that the initial act outlawing witchcraft in Scotland had been passed, but James went so far as to write a treatise on 'Daemonologie', after taking an active part in a notorious witch trial of 1590. Held at North Berwick, east of the capital, this involved an alleged coven accused of conjuring up a storm in an attempt to sink a ship carrying the king and queen. Many of the more than 70 individuals implicated were subjected to hideous torture in order to extract confessions.

Nearly 4,000 people in Scotland, mainly women, are known to have been tried for witchcraft before the repeal of the act in 1736, and a third of these cases took place in Edinburgh and the Lothians. Hundreds were put to death, generally by strangulation at the stake, followed by burning, on the city's Castlehill. Contrary to popular belief, they were very rarely ducked in the Nor' Loch first, to see whether they floated. The grisly farce of 'witch pricking' was, however, a common means of establishing culpability.

Though some victims seem to have been guilty of little more than an acid tongue, many of those denounced were women using folk remedies and herbal medicine who had the gift of healing – and who were believed capable of using their powers for evil ends. It is to these gravely misjudged healers that the ambivalent little memorial known as the Witches' Fountain is dedicated. The Art Nouveau relief was sculpted in 1894 by John Duncan, a mystical figure who spoke of hearing 'faerie music' while he worked.

Address Castlehill, Edinburgh, EH1 2ND | Getting there Lothian Buses 9, 23 or 27 to George IV Bridge. The fountain is on a wall just to the right of the entrance to the Castle Esplanade. | Tip The 5-storey building to which the fountain is attached was originally the city's main reservoir, holding 1.7 million gallons of water. It's now occupied by the Tartan Weaving Mill, where visitors can observe weavers working at looms. Plans are under way to transform it into a combined retail facility and educational heritage attraction.

111 World's End

The limits of a gated community

For today's pedestrians, the 'lang Scots mile' from Castlehill to Abbey Strand is an unbroken thoroughfare, but it wasn't always so easily negotiable. The Royal Mile was completely blocked, for a significant period of history, by the obstacle of the Netherbow Port gateway, at the point where the High Street joins the Canongate. To many people within the confines of the city, this marked the limit of their known universe. Exiting might not have been so difficult, but everyone entering the gate, visitors and residents alike, had to pay a toll, which greatly restricted poorer citizens' prospects of trips into the world outside. And so, the story goes, the area just inside its main eastern portal gained the nickname of World's End.

The Netherbow was one of six ports in the enclosing walls, defences that were extended and strengthened after 1513, when the disastrous Scottish defeat at the Battle of Flodden hastened the threat of an English invasion. As the eastern flank was most vulnerable to attack, the Netherbow was heavily fortified, but since it was also the entry point for royalty coming from Holyrood Palace, the gateway was made appropriately grand and decorative. In 1606 it was remodelled in imitation of the Porte Saint-Honoré in Paris, with a tall, spired clock tower above the main archway, flanked by round bastions with conical roofs. This was done in anticipation of the imminent arrival in the city of King James VI, who had left in 1603 to assume the throne of England, promising to return to his Scottish home every three years. In the event the expatriate monarch made it back only once, in 1617.

Though its former site is discreetly commemorated, the majestic gateway itself is long gone, demolished in 1764 to improve traffic flow. The World's End tag now lives on in an adjacent pub, a good place for anyone who needs a fortifying drink before venturing into the wild blue yonder.

Address High Street, EH1 1TB, at the crossroads with St Mary's Street/Jeffrey Street. The site of the Netherbow Port is outlined by brass plates in the roadway. | Getting there Lothian Buses 35 to the High Street | Hours World's End pub: Sun–Thu 11am–11pm, Fri & Sat 11am–midnight (www.belhavenpubs.co.uk) | Tip The Scottish Storytelling Centre at 43–45 High Street is a stylish arts venue, with a varied programme including live storytelling, as well as an all-day café. A carved plaque and bell from the Netherbow Port are preserved in the building.

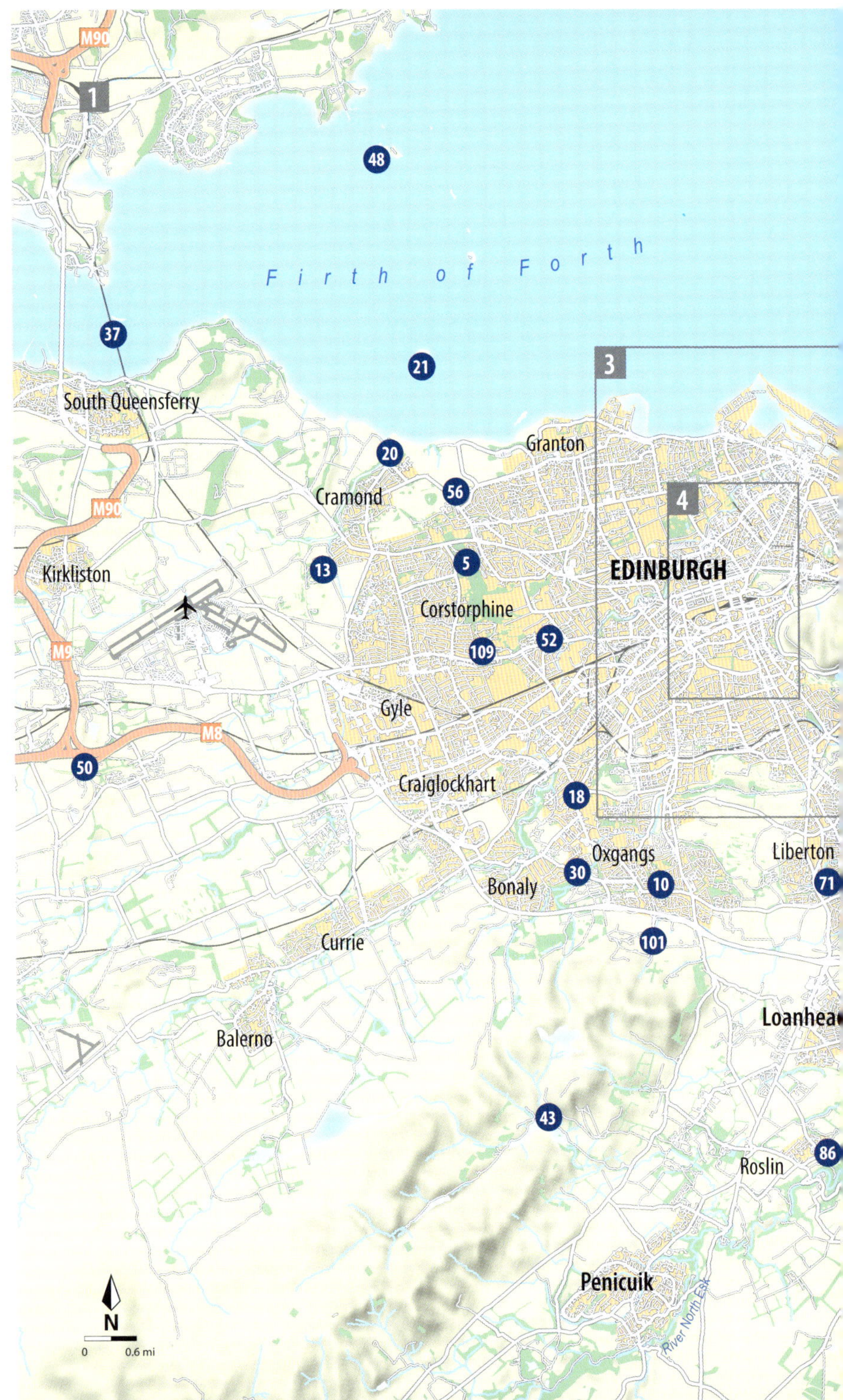
M90
1
48
Firth of Forth
37
21
3
South Queensferry
Granton
20
Cramond
56
M90
4
Kirkliston
13
5
EDINBURGH
Corstorphine
M9
109
52
Gyle
M8
50
Craiglockhart
18
Oxgangs
Liberton
30
10
71
Bonaly
101
Currie
Balerno
43
86
Roslin
Penicuik
River North Esk
N
0
0.6 mi

2
16
Prestonpans
87
79
80
Portobello
Musselburgh
70
Tranent
Craigmillar
Monktonhall
85
19
River Esk
Gilmerton
41
Ormiston
Pencaitland
Dalkeith
44
Bonnyrigg
Mayfield
55
Pathhead
Newtongrange
N
0
0.6 mi

3

Port of Leith

108

107 59

Commercial Street

NEWHAVEN

TRINITY

LEITH

105

Leith Links

Ferry Road

4

Leith Walk

35

Inverleith Park

97

61

3

NEW TOWN

London Road

77

Queensferry Road

66

Willowbrae Road

23

22

24

OLD TOWN

Holyrood Park

92

49

28 102

The Meadows

Duddingston Loch

BRUNTSFIELD

17

4

26

93

MORNINGSIDE

Cluny Gardens

BLACKFORD

19

Craigmillar Castle Park

6

Liberton Road

46

LIBERTON

N

0 0,3 mi

Comiston Road

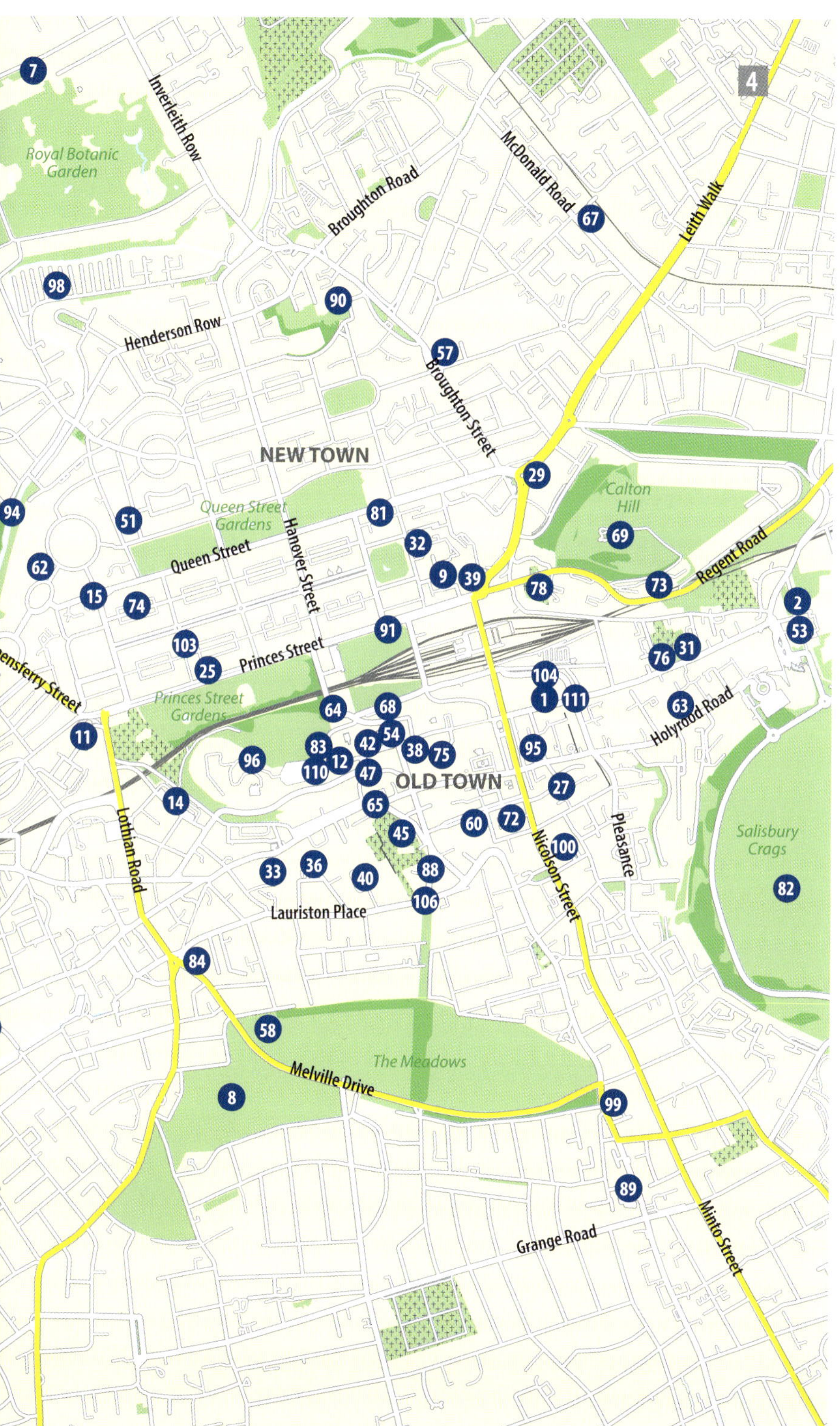

4
Royal Botanic Garden
Inverleith Row
Broughton Road
McDonald Road
Leith Walk
Henderson Row
Broughton Street
NEW TOWN
Calton Hill
Queen Street Gardens
Queen Street
Hanover Street
Regent Road
Princes Street
Queensferry Street
Princes Street Gardens
Holyrood Road
OLD TOWN
Lothian Road
Pleasance
Nicolson Street
Salisbury Crags
Lauriston Place
The Meadows
Melville Drive
Grange Road
Minto Street

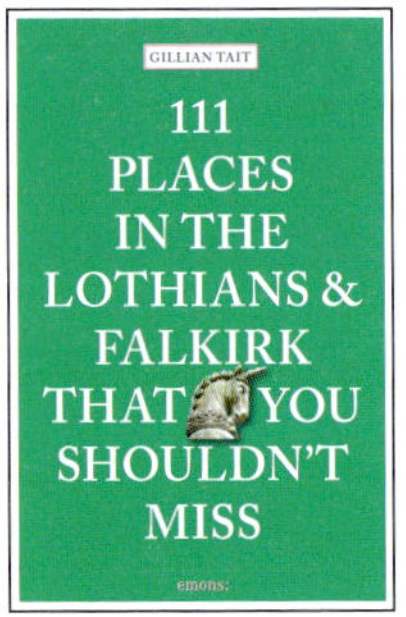

Gillian Tait
111 Places in the Lothians and Falkirk That You Shouldn't Miss
ISBN 978-3-7408-1569-1

Gillian Tait
111 Places in Fife That You Shouldn't Miss
ISBN 978-3-7408-1740-4

Tom Shields, Gillian Tait
111 Places in Glasgow That You Shouldn't Miss
ISBN 978-3-7408-2237-8

Julia Goodfellow-Smith
111 Places in Swansea That You Shouldn't Miss
ISBN 978-3-7408-2065-7

David Taylor
111 Places in Newcastle That You Shouldn't Miss
ISBN 978-3-7408-1043-6

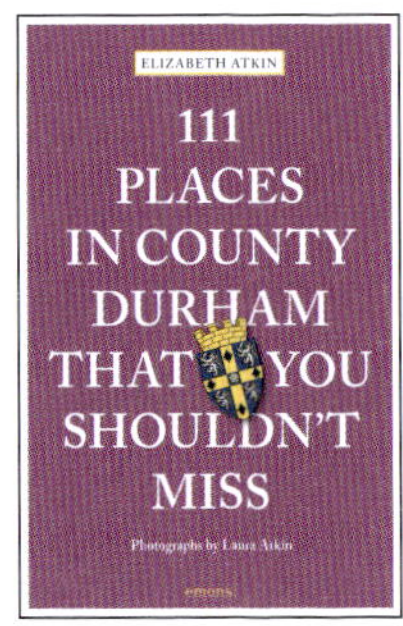

Elizabeth Atkin, Laura Atkin
111 Places in County Durham That You Shouldn't Miss
ISBN 978-3-7408-1426-7

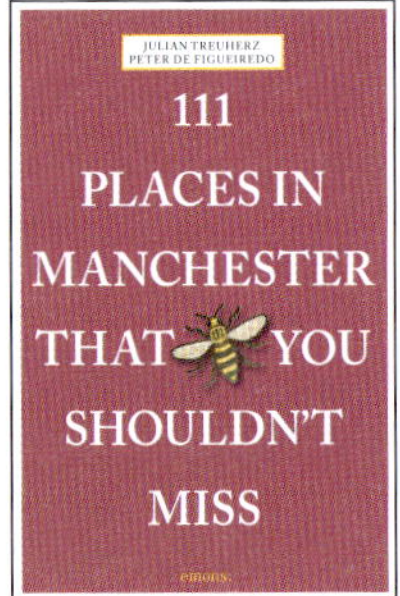

Julian Treuherz, Peter de Figueiredo
111 Places in Manchester That You Shouldn't Miss
ISBN 978-3-7408-2645-1

Julian Treuherz, Peter de Figueiredo
111 Places in Liverpool That You Shouldn't Miss
ISBN 978-3-7408-2515-7

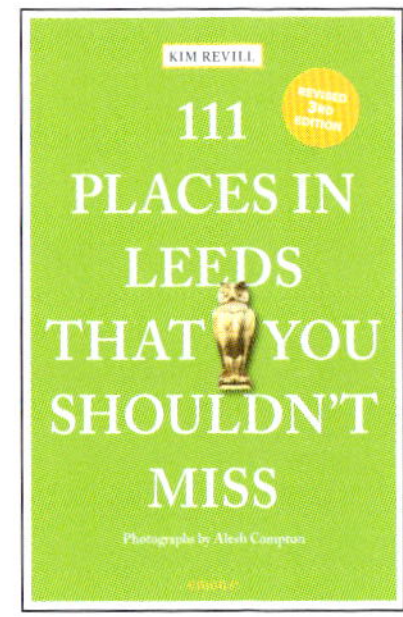

Kim Revill, Alesh Compton
111 Places in Leeds That You Shouldn't Miss
ISBN 978-3-7408-2059-6

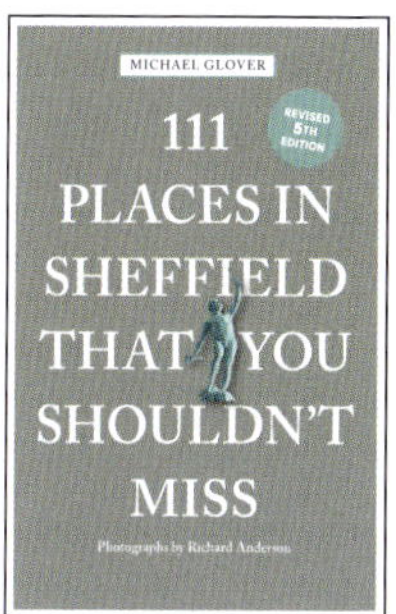

Michael Glover,
Richard Anderson
111 Places in Sheffield
That You Shouldn't Miss
ISBN 978-3-7408-2348-1

David Taylor
111 Places in Northumberland
That You Shouldn't Miss
ISBN 978-3-7408-1792-3

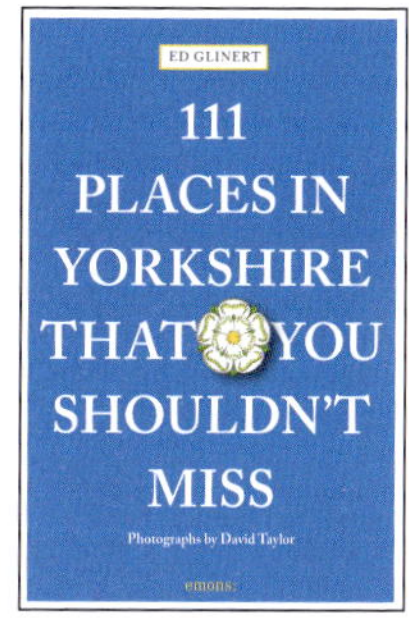

Ed Glinert, David Taylor
111 Places in Yorkshire
That You Shouldn't Miss
ISBN 978-3-7408-1167-9

Ed Glinert, Karin Tearle
111 Places in Essex
That You Shouldn't Miss
ISBN 978-3-7408-1593-6

Solange Berchemin
111 Places in the Lake District
That You Shouldn't Miss
ISBN 978-3-7408-2404-4

Alexandra Loske
111 Places in Brighton and
Lewes That You Shouldn't Miss
ISBN 978-3-7408-1727-5

Catriona Neil, Adrian Spalding
111 Places in Cornwall
That You Shouldn't Miss
ISBN 978-3-7408-1901-9

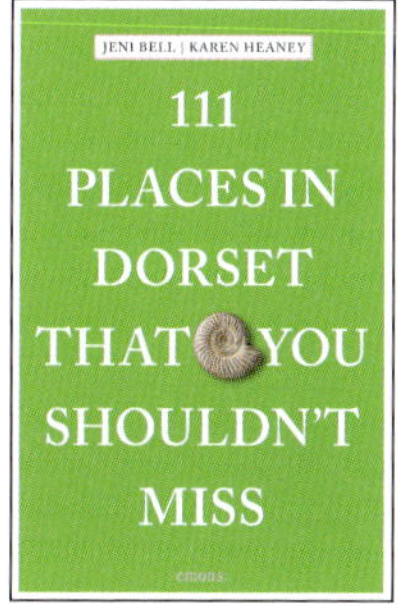

Jeni Bell, Karen Heaney
111 Places in Dorset
That You Shouldn't Miss
ISBN 978-3-7408-2146-3

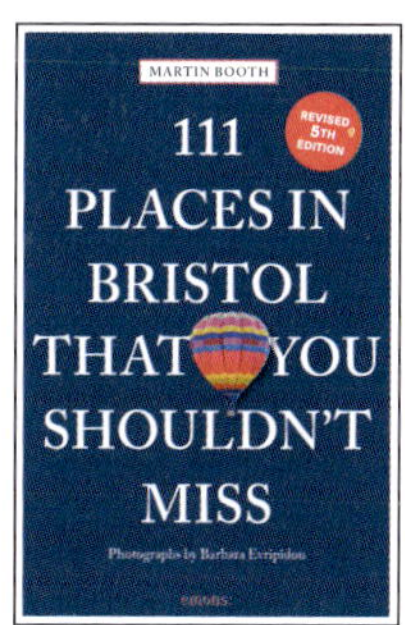

Martin Booth, Barbara Evripidou
111 Places in Bristol
That You Shouldn't Miss
ISBN 978-3-7408-2512-6

Martin Booth, Barbara Evripidou
111 Places for Kids in Bristol That You Shouldn't Miss
ISBN 978-3-7408-1665-0

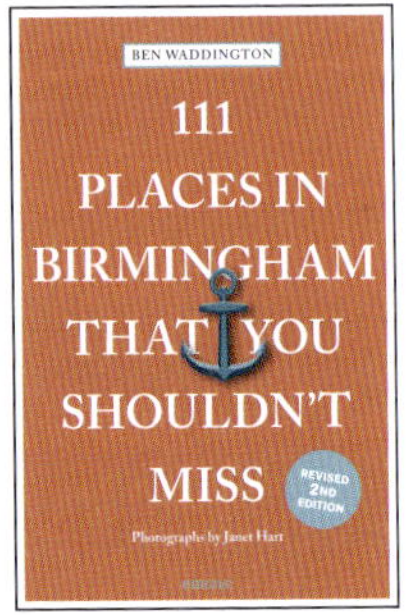

Ben Waddington, Janet Hart
111 Places in Birmingham That You Shouldn't Miss
ISBN 978-3-7408-2268-2

Ed Glinert, David Taylor
111 Places in Oxford That You Shouldn't Miss
ISBN 978-3-7408-1990-3

Rosalind Horton,
Sally Simmons, Guy Snape
111 Places in Cambridge That You Shouldn't Miss
ISBN 978-3-7408-2376-4

John Sykes, Birgit Weber
111 Places in London That You Shouldn't Miss
ISBN 978-3-7408-2379-5

Alicia Edwards
111 Places for Kids in London That You Shouldn't Miss
ISBN 978-3-7408-2196-8

Michael Glover, Benedict Flett
111 Hidden Art Treasures in London That You Shouldn't Miss
ISBN 978-3-7408-1576-9

Terry Philpot, Karin Tearle
111 Literary Places in London That You Shouldn't Miss
ISBN 978-3-7408-1954-5

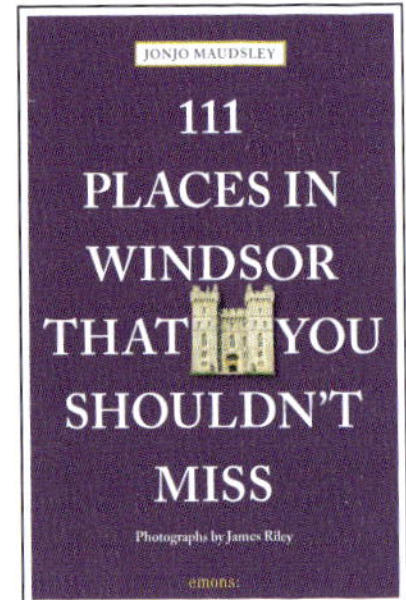

Jonjo Maudsley, James Riley
111 Places in Windsor That You Shouldn't Miss
ISBN 978-3-7408-2009-1

Acknowledgements

Many friends have made useful suggestions that have greatly helped me in my selection of these fascinating places, and I'm particularly grateful to the following: Ben Tindall, Henry Noltie, Susan Ross, Vicki Clifford, Fionna Carlisle, John McGurk, Stuart Clark, Howard Bell, Giulia Dawson and Bob Martin. I would also like to thank Alistair Layzell for his consistently reassuring advice, and Norma Armstrong (St Margaret's Restalrig), Margaretanne Duggan (Gilmerton Cove), Michael Durnan (Lauriston Castle), Ian Gardner (Rosslyn Chapel), Darryl Martin (St Cecilia's Hall) and David McLeod (Surgeons' Hall Museums) for their kind assistance with access and photography. Above all, my heartfelt gratitude goes to my former husband Julian, without whose patient, generous and practical support this book could not have been written.

Gillian Tait was born in Edinburgh, and grew up in other parts of Scotland. She studied art history and painting conservation at the universities of Edinburgh and London respectively, and worked for many years in the museum sector in Scotland, England and the USA. More recently she has occupied her time as a writer, editor and photographer, while indulging her passions for travel, singing and performing in opera, operetta and musical theatre, and improving her Italian. *111 Places in Edinburgh That You Shouldn't Miss* was her first book in this series, and she subsequently contributed to *111 Places in Glasgow That You Shouldn't Miss* as photographer and editor. She has since produced two further *111 Places* guides as both author and photographer, covering *Fife* and, most recently, *the Lothians and Falkirk*. She has lived in the heart of Edinburgh's Old Town for nearly 40 years.